PRAISE FOR *CASHING IN!*

Sellers, buyers, and business advisors have acclaimed Cashing In! as a superb primer on the ins and outs of middle market business sale. Written by successful merger and acquisition guru Deborah Douglas, this book brims with almost evangelical passion to ensure that business owners gain every edge possible to claim top rewards in sale.

"I didn't want to put it down...conversational and clever writing style, filled with helpful information on the complexities of getting the best price for your company."

Dee Joyner, Senior Vice President, Commerce Bank

"Extremely interesting...an easy read full of valuable information."

John Lewis, former business owner

"*Cashing In!* is a 'must read' for everyone building and some day planning to sell their American Dream. Not only does it give the 'how to' and 'what to do' when you are ready to sell— it helps you start preparing now so you will be ready when that right time comes.

Judy Meador, Publisher, *St. Louis Small Business Monthly*

"No numbers, no high finance – just fun reading with plenty of deal savvy that'll make money!"

Jim O'Donnell, Chairman & CEO, Capital for Business

"*Cashing In!* is a must-read for middle market business owners. It is a truly outstanding all-around guide to building and maximizing business value."

Keith Guller, President & CEO, Essex Industries

"Business sellers, buyers, and advisors will strike gold with this book... A witty, down-to-earth manual for successful middle market mergers and acquisitions."

Dennis Coleman, President & CEO, St. Louis County Economic Council

"A quick read, anecdote-filled, on the ins and outs of deal making...serves up valuable insights on negotiating strategy and psychology to help sellers side-step deal-breaking land mines, while extracting top dollar for their companies."

Robert Grace, Editor and Associate Publisher, Plastics News

"Outstanding guide, full of practical and useful advice for all business owners (and their financial advisors) for maximizing values."

Robert Spindel, CEO, Paradyme Financial Advisors

"Anyone contemplating the sale of a business ought to read this book."

Charles Ruprecht, Consultant and Retired CEO
Hussmann Refrigeration

"This book is a great primer for the enlightened business owner... when the game is finally over, the only value of a business is the price someone will pay for it."

Michael Gerber, author of *E-Myth*

"A page turner…I picked up important tips…thank you!"

"a savvy primer on how to sell a business… Filled with real life examples, funny stories, and invaluable tips. I highly recommend it."

"… a gifted writer. *Cashing In!* is filled with practical and valuable insights on how to sell one's business. If our clients, who come to us for investment counsel, had come through Douglas, they would have had more wealth for us to manage!"

"Anyone who will ever buy or sell a company will benefit from this book…a masterful study of the art and science of selling a business."

"Very well written and easy to understand…includes both excellent examples of firsthand experiences and memorable quotes… I am happy to recommend it!"

"Debbie Douglas provides a candid and revealing look at what the sale of a middle market company is really all about. A great read for any business owner or advisor!"

"In a time of economic volatility, this book goes right to the heart of what it REALLY takes to drive business value. Great practical advice for business owners!"

Thomas Cook, Corporate Counsel, Insituform

Acknowledgements:

Many thanks to the kind souls who generously gave their time and wisdom in early review of this book.

Thanks to Billie Emerick for the long hours of support and ever-smiling goodwill in the effort.

Thanks to my publisher, Tom Costello, for a great helping hand at every turn.

Thanks to the superb people at Douglas Group for all of your advice and encouragement.

Thanks to my clients for many years of great experiences and warm relationships.

Thanks to my husband, Rick Aselage, and daughter Lara Douglas for reading, critiquing and cheering.

CASHING IN!

Selling Your Business for Maximum Price

BY
DEBORAH L. DOUGLAS
Managing Director

Douglas Group
St. Louis, MO

CASHING IN!
Selling Your Business for Maximum Price

ISBN: 1-891231-79-0

Library of Congress Control Number:
2002104781

Word Association Publishers
205 Fifth Avenue
Tarentum, PA 15084
800-827-7903
www.wordassociation.com

Ordering Information

Toll-free telephone orders: 800-827-7903. Have your credit card number ready.

Fax orders: 724-226-3974.

On-line orders: orders@wordassociation.com

To contact Deborah Douglas:
731 Old Frontenac Square
St. Louis, Missouri 63131
341-991-5150
ddouglas@douglasgroup.net

For a signed copy, send $15.00 + $4.00 S/H to the above address.

This book may also be ordered from your local bookseller.
ISBN 1-891231-79-0

Online ordering at:
www.amazon.com
www.bn.com

Contents

Introduction

Advance Preparation/Building Value

The Selling Process

Negotiating Techniques

Appendices

Introduction

PRIME OBJECTIVE

My company's business is the sale of businesses. We handle the ultimate cash-in for a business—often representing literally a lifetime of someone's hard work. We believe that what we do is incredibly important. Business owners get one chance to sell their businesses well, and only one. We make sure that this single one-time event plays out to the optimal reward for the business owner.

The prime objective is to sell a business and, in so doing, to create maximum wealth for the seller.

We find the right buyer to make the perfect match. We solidify wealth, rewarding the entrepreneur for years of business risk. We find new capital and enhanced managerial support for vigorous growth of the business into new directions. We create opportunity for talented new leadership. We look for combinations where the sum of the parts can be greater than the standalone elements. We are passionate about what we do, because we believe that what we do is fundamentally good: supportive and nurturing to the very backbone of our free economic society.

This book is written for business owners, and for aspiring business owners, whose ultimate objective is to make money through business ownership. It is written from a philosophical perspective built around the belief that profit is a wholesome motive, and that free enterprise is a complex and wonderfully self-regulating system that causes good things to happen.

My teenaged daughter once explained my sociopolitical philosophy, in her own words, to a group of friends: "You have to understand my mom's core philosophy. She thinks that healthy selfishness is really good for the world."

The true heroes of economic good are business owners. Business owners create ever-improving goods and services for our use. They create jobs for honest workers, and opportunities for such workers' growth and prosperity. They raise and fill buildings to house their enterprises. They put tax dollars in our nation's public coffers to be used to serve and protect us.

A Russian immigrant friend of mine has his own definition of free enterprise, which offers an interesting perspective from a once hardcore socialist. He says that free enterprise is "shameless exploitation for the common good."

Business owners roll the dice every day, risking everything to build the enterprise. They work long hours, and borrow money for capital. They pledge their homes and everything they have to lenders. They often put their family name on the enterprise, as if to pledge that the business will survive, or their good name will go down with it.

There comes a time in the life of every business owner when he or she begins to think about sale. Business owners want (and deserve) to cash in on their life's work. They want to secure the fruits of their labors, and to step back from the risks of ownership. It is time for someone new—a buyer—to assume the leadership mantle.

This is the story of how to realize the ultimate profit in that final "cashing in" exchange.

THE AMERICAN DREAM

Much of working America shares a bit of THE American Dream. The American Dream swells and contracts in popularity, as is true with most important ideas. Fortunately though, so much of our economy is built upon it that it is unlikely ever to disappear.

It goes something like this: Hard-working Person has an idea for a product or service that could sell. Person doesn't have much money to kick off the idea and turn it into a real business, but Person is determined. Person gets creative. Person hocks the house, borrows from relatives, and starts on a shoestring— maybe with a basement for an office and a garage for a warehouse.

Business takes over the house and family. Every square foot has paraphernalia. Every family member kicks in some bit of help. Product sells. Slowly at first. Then, after what seems like eons but probably spans a mere six to eighteen months, there's enough value or enough volume to justify (in fact, to require) a real outside-of-the-home place of business. More people are needed to help, more stuff is needed, and it simply can't fit in the basement and garage anymore.

Company competes, grows, and flourishes. Each layer of growth brings new problems and traumas, but each challenge is, in the end, successfully met.

One day, Super Corporation knocks on the door and says, "You're ready for the big leagues. We want—we NEED—to buy your company." (How many movies have we seen with a piece of this story?)

A few months later the deal is closed and the story hits the front page of the local paper. Entrepreneur strikes it rich. No more risk. No more worry. The cash is in the bank! Creativity, courage, and lots of hard work pay off with glittering wealth and glory!

Last year, there were almost 980,000 new businesses launched in America. There were another 100,000 businesses purchased. There were 315,000 new patents applied for, and countless more new products and services launched without benefit of proprietary legal protection.

The American Dream is alive and well—and in a great many cases it really can and does come true.

OWN A COMPANY—NOT A JOB

Author and speaker Michael Gerber, perhaps most famous originally for his writing of *The E-Myth*, is a favorite of mine. *The E-Myth* is an insightful exploration of the entrepreneurial endeavor, with fascinating observations about the personality traits common and even necessary to the successful business builder. Gerber challenges entrepreneurs to keep in mind the purpose of building a business, and not to lose focus on the ultimate objective.

I've enjoyed all of Gerber's books, but after reading the first two, I had the pleasure of hearing him speak. At the outset of his talk, he looked at the audience with great intensity, and shouted, **"The only purpose in this world in owning a company is to SELL IT! If you can't sell it, you don't own a business—you own a JOB!"**

Naturally, as a highly paid expert in the sale of businesses, I like that thought. However, he is not telling all business owners that they should sell their companies tomorrow. He is saying that as long as your business relies on you, as a worker, to produce income, it is not a freestanding asset with substantive value. It is, instead, a glorified job.

Admittedly the amount of "glory" in business ownership is highly questionable. If you want fame, become a rock star, an athlete, or a politician.

For most entrepreneurs the top priority is not fame or glory. Typically the entrepreneur seeks independence and financial success. Neither of those things is ever maximized until the company is able to "live" without daily owner maintenance.

When you do sell your company, if you have managed to build a real productive asset, you will realize many times more benefit when cashing in. When the company you have built can produce sales, recruit and retain talented people, and consistently deliver quality products or services—all without your personal hands-on touch, you have created value. You have added to the economic well-being of your community. You have also freed yourself. Great work!

Regardless of when or how you may choose to cash in on the value that you build, remember that your company isn't "done" until it's a living, breathing entity that is self-sustaining.

Some years ago when I was a young CPA, my firm represented a man who owned a thriving mid-sized company with about $30 million in annual sales. The owner received an unsolicited offer to purchase the company for $40 million in cash, with the request for a one-year contract for employment, during which time the new owner could transition management to a replacement CEO. The owner passed on the offer, because he thought that he might want to continue working for up to three to five *more years, and he worried that a one-year time frame might be too limiting. Fourteen months after the offer had been made, the owner suffered a stroke. He was out of the office entirely for the next eight months. Production problems surfaced. Sales staff became frustrated with product failures and distracted with worries about who might emerge as the new CEO. Good people began leaving. By the time the owner returned (even then, only on a part-time basis), sales had dropped to around $12 million per year (less than half of the pre-stroke volume), and the company was losing money at an astounding pace. After six months back at work, still fighting health problems and finding it extremely taxing to try to rebuild, the owner decided to sell. Unfortunately the company was no longer desirable. Enterprise value, as a multiple of earnings, had gone from $40 million to zero. The owner sold assets, liquidated the corporation, and barely cleared enough to cover debt. His $40 million in value was lost, all because he was worried about keeping his job.*

Don't fall into the trap of "I'm old enough, I've worked hard, and the world owes me a living." It doesn't. *It was here first.*

Build your company, make it strong, and create value! Ownership of a saleable company is the ultimate job security.

AdvancePreparation/
Building Value

THE BENEFIT OF THE NICHE

Most business owners begin with a vision. They may not frame it in their mind as a "vision"; but nonetheless, they have one. At the core, the vision begins with some void or weakness in the marketplace, which the aspiring new owner thinks he can competitively fill with a new product or service.

Rock Sathre started a manufacturing company in a small rented garage. He manufactured custom subassemblies for various customers. He made his own tooling, designed to enhance production quality and to solve special problems for his customers. He knew he could provide competitive services, because he could solve certain types of manufacturing problems that others couldn't. Industrial Custom Products was formed.

Nancy Friedman complained to her insurance agent about his horrible telephone reception and service. At his request she came in a week later and spent an hour telling his staff how to do a better job in responding to customers on the phone. Results were so good that she then had several follow-up calls from friends of his, asking her to do the same for their companies. It didn't take long for her to say, "This is a need in the marketplace which I can fill." Her company, Telephone Doctor, was formed.

The initial vision for a business is generally a focused concept for filling a needed niche. Over time, this initial clarity of the enterprise vision naturally changes and evolves. Opportunities come along, which, although not the original focus of the business, seem to offer short-term help to building revenue levels. The owner tells himself he is "expanding" into other areas. The incidental new business that happens along is happily folded in as increased revenue, without much scrutiny as to its relative fit with the initial concept. Focus becomes blurred.

These are natural responses to normal patterns of growth and evolution. Unfortunately these "natural" patterns can be dangerous. Growth without focus can be hazardous to your company's health.

Strategic buyers—the ones who pay most dearly for the select enterprises that they want—search for FOCUS. They want the niche player, who has carved out a special spot where he is king.

So what is a "niche"? What does that actually mean in form and appearance?

For the manufacturer it may mean that you are the only provider of a patented technology or a "family" of patented technologies. For a distributor it may mean that you are THE supplier of 70% of a narrow given category of product in the United States. For a service company it may mean that you have a solid reputation as the best provider of a single service. For a retailer it may mean that you have the most complete stock of a particular well-defined product category. It may be a focus on customers whom you understand, an extended service capability that perfectly fills a need, or an element of quality that you alone have perfected.

Aristotle Onassis said that the secret of all business is to know something that nobody else knows. That advantage is what gives you focus.

When buyers see it, they want it. Your margins of profit are higher than others because of your niche position. Your competition will have far greater trouble displacing you. You have the momentum of success in one focused area, which is likely to build naturally upon itself and multiply, in continuation of a solid trend line.

In the entire world of attributes that add value to businesses, there is no one element as important as FOCUS.

"Put all of your eggs in one basket   then watch the basket." Mark Twain.

We represented the owner of a plastics manufacturing company who was eager to sell his business and who was very excited about his niche. He informed me that he had not only one, but TWO niches! Even better than one! His company was a leading manufacturer of every plastic part imaginable for the snowmobile industry, from fenders to dash panels to mirror trim. They had the best clients in the world in this segment, and they proudly worked to know more than anyone in the world about snowmobile production issues, market demand, and even timing for their customers' production needs.

At the same time, the company was also fast becoming one of the top producers of anti-static packaging in the United States. These two markets accounted for around 80% of the company's business while the other 20% was somewhat ad hoc. Ad hoc in this case did not mean unimportant. The company cared meticulously for all of its customers, and had many special little pet products. As a result, profits were great, customer relationships were excellent, and we were thrilled to take this fine company to market.

We researched and probed and carefully screened to identify the "best" prospective buyers. Packaging concerns were paying great prices for acquisitions. Our client sold anti-static packaging products to the computer and telecommunications giants, and the major players in this market were cool and polished developers of the mega-sized customer account. They recognized promising value in our client, particularly in one clever product design and in its niche development of budding anti-static solutions. Thus they found the company very interesting. However, when viewed in total, one after another concluded that it was not quite a natural fit. "We love the anti-static packaging niche these people have carved out, and it could be a great complement to our other product offerings. But...is that a snowmobile fender?"

The recreational vehicle types were a hardier, more free-wheeling crowd, with great appreciation for our client's understand-

ing of their customers. "These guys really know their stuff. Look at these ingenious handguards that won't break, even at one hundred degrees below! But...what in the world are those anti-static people doing? Production people wearing hairnets and booties seem a little outside of our range."

The two business segments could not be split apart, because they shared too many people, too much capital equipment base, and all of their space. The company was still great and commanded a good price, but if either one of the segments alone had represented a vast share of the business, the company would probably have brought at least 25% more.

Is there risk in focus? Sure. But it creates power and life and targeted drive, which is usually worth the risk.

As one of my Texan clients once put it, "If you're gonna be great, you gotta figure out where you're goin', and you gotta commit. There's nothin' in the middle of the road but yellow stripes and dead armadillos."

KNOW THYSELF

Every company that survives over an extended period of time has elements of special genius that give it the genetic capability for survival. The elemental genius of the business is its unique collection of special attributes that make it competitively superior. Such attributes range from product mix to quality, price, service, location, and all of the aspects of the business that differentiate it in the eyes of the customer.

Regardless of the nature of the business, every enterprise faces competition. Customers choose one business as their preference over another alternative, and the chosen one survives. The alternatives are not necessarily parallel competitors, but, in one form or another, the customer always does have choices. Inevitably your customers managed before you and will find a way to manage without you. However, in every sales dollar you generate, they have chosen to survive with you.

In all of our years of experience in examining and becoming intimately familiar with client sellers, we have been repeatedly surprised to find out how many of our clients have lost sight of their fundamental elements of value to their customers.

Business is like riding a bicycle. If you stop pedaling, you're going to fall over.

Stay focused. Keep adapting. Keep your eye on the big picture. One of our favorite strategic analysis tools, good to use even far in advance of sale, is the SWOT analysis. SWOT is an acronym for Strengths, Weaknesses, Opportunities, and Threats. The analysis is a self-assessment, which is valuable in part because it encourages the introspection necessary to fully assess competitive and market position, and in part because it invites forward consideration of future possibilities. It is an extremely helpful self-view and is often one of our earliest analyses of a seller client. It also tends to closely mirror the study most buyers will make as they contemplate possible purchase.

If you, by the time of sale, can comfortably speak to your true position in your market, and your strategy for coping with the future (both opportunities and threats), you will find yourself: (a) more profitable and more secure, and (b) in fine form for astute presentation to buyers.

FAMILY MATTERS

Business owners often agonize about family succession issues. They have a natural desire to give their children a head start in life. They want to let their children pick up at the summit of what they themselves have accomplished.

There is no more natural desire for a parent. However, beware the pitfalls.

- Second-generation business people often do not have the talent or skills to pick up in the next stage of the business evolution. It is very difficult to build entrepreneurial instincts into a child growing up as son or daughter of the boss. If children don't have the raw capability, you will harm both their psyche and their inheritance by putting them in a position to ultimately fail.

- As you plan for business ownership transition, keep in mind that kids working in the business view things quite differently from kids outside of the business. Family ownership can be an enormous source of sibling conflict. The kids in the business will think, "I helped to build this business. I was toiling away for all of these years, and I have earned a greater reward than my siblings outside."

The kids not in the business, in response, will think, "You had a job given to you for all of those years. You got the company car and the benefits. I, on the other hand, had to make my own way in the world. You have had disproportionate advantages."

• If you think it's complicated to contemplate sale with one set of family members, that's a day in the park in comparison to the third or later generations, with multiple family units involved. If you have more than one family member involved, and there are likely to be multiple kids as heirs, develop a mechanism now to shift control to one or two key operators. Do not leave it to be decided and agreed upon by those increasingly diverse next-generation beneficiaries.

We did some expert-witness testimony for a family where three siblings worked in the business, and several third-generation kids were employed by the company as well. As the years passed, the family segmented into two factions, dramatically at odds. One wanted to sell and one did not. The non-sellers obstructed sale in every way possible. The bitterness and unreasonableness on the part of both sides was unbelievable.

The matter finally went to court, and a judge ruled that sale was the only possible option. Unfortunately however, that judgment was late in coming. By that time, the owners of the company had diminished its value to about one-third of its former glory. In the meantime, multiple lawsuits had been filed, a five-generation family vacation property (owned by all) had been sold in a fit of rage by the managing trustee, and a competitive business had been formed by two of the third-generation kids. The family relationship was destroyed, and the value of the business with it.

Family ownership transition is risky business. Think twice about your priorities before you gift or "sell" to a child, and think ten times before you sell to more than one.

TIMING YOUR MOVE

Owners have a tendency to contemplate sale when they are nervous or tired or both. Naturally it is most tempting to exit when you're less than pumped up about your future. When two semi-major disasters have fallen from the sky, and sixteen more have threatened, the owner begins to think about getting out while the getting's good. The ever-present risk of business ownership begins to weigh heavily.

In the immortal words of one of our clients: "Every time I think I'm winning the rat race...along comes a faster rat!"

When is the best time to sell in order to maximize value? Of course, it's just before you get to the top of the hill. It's just after the best string of good times the Company has ever had. It's the year of the best success ever.

Part of the timing issue revolves around the economic prognosis. Most business owners wouldn't even pretend to be great economic gurus. I once heard Federal Reserve Chairman Alan Greenspan speaking to a group of business owners. In his introductory remarks, he said, *"I guess I should warn you: if I turn out to be particularly clear, you've probably misunderstood what I've said."* The economy is complex and almost impossible to forecast reliably. However, most business owners do tend to have a fairly reliable instinct for the short-term future of their own business niche.

For the long-stable, growing operation, the "best time" may be hard to anticipate. Although the clear objective is to sell just before any downturn, it can be difficult to predict when a downturn will come. As an economist friend of mine puts it, *"You really can't tell who's swimming naked until the tide goes out."* However, any reasonably strong recent history will serve you well and pay off. Buyers generally will feel they should pay a multiple of the last running twelve months of profits. If you've been downturning for the past two years but you're hoping they'll pay for an average of the past five years' performance, you're kidding yourself. If, at the other extreme, your most recent year is a complete oddity, with super performance for the first and only time in history, you will have a credibility issue. This problem is actually not quite as serious, in that a reasonable likelihood of continuation at the new high levels will make buyers dismiss the bygone lackluster years as irrelevant. However, buyers will need to understand enough about your business to believe in the profitable continuation of the upturn.

The business life cycle for the single-owner enterprise often runs something like this:

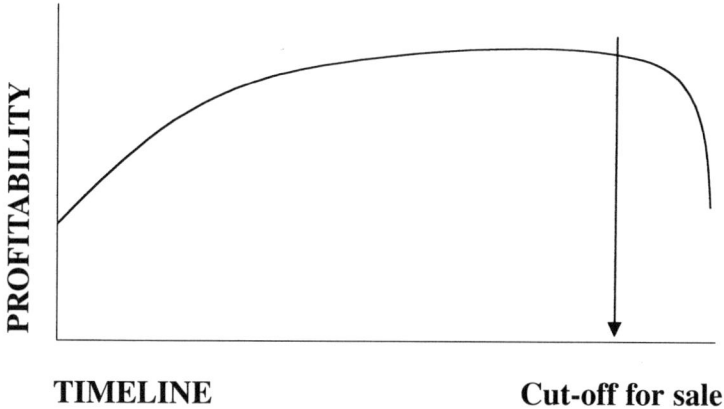

TIMELINE   **Cut-off for sale**

Unfortunately all too many owners delay action on possible sale until the last possible moment, when they've come too close to falling off the cliff. They know they should sell and they know that value is declining, but they're afraid to make their move. They procrastinate, due to fear that perhaps it's too soon to relax, or they cling to unrealistic hope for the magical comeback.

My teenaged son is a wrestler. One of the young men on his team last year suffered losses repeatedly and painfully. After one particularly disheartening match, we saw the assistant coach give the youngster twenty minutes of pep talk to cheer and encourage him. It was between rounds, and the kids were taking a break, so my son sat beside his father and me, and observed the pep talk. Afterward, he shook his head slowly, and said, "What if, right at this very moment, he already is living up to his full potential?"

There have been times when I thought that words to similar effect might be the kindest revelation I could make to a particularly struggling prospective client. If you find yourself running a company on a downhill track, do yourself a favor by recognizing the issue and taking decisive action. Sell before the downhill slope becomes too steep.

Advice from one of our sage clients: *"Eat right. Exercise. Die anyway."* Life is too short.

There is a time in the life of every problem when it's big enough to see, but small enough to solve. Move then.

Another common misstep we see in timing involves the company that has a new high-tech product about to unfold. Biotech and information-technology companies often face this position. The best moment for sale in this environment is inevitably after proof of viability and function, but BEFORE the attempt to go full force with the new product to the broad market. These companies are actually the most sensitive and volatile of all with respect to timing for sale. The promise or the hope of enormous success is often far more valuable than the final outcome. Buyers will bid for the chance to own a hit.

The upstart development company which is great at managing through the creative torment of early product innovation is rarely capable of the rigorous business discipline required in taking a fast-evolving product to market maturity. Also, in almost every case of innovative product development, time is of the essence. Even with patent protections, competitors will look for ways to introduce similar products. Some may even trounce directly on proprietary patent rights, and dare the developer to spend the time and money to try to stop them. Regardless of how it may come to pass, expect competitive energy to surface quickly around any successful new product.

The high-tech developer of new products can make fast profit and avoid enormous risk by courting competitive bids for purchase, just before time for the all-out sales/production effort. Unfortunately however, the inventive, entrepreneurial personality, nurtured with some technological success, can become excessively optimistic. Early stage developers often don't appreciate the risks and the pitfalls of rapid growth. They think they can sort it out as they go, but alas, the vast majority fail. It's often worth a sacrifice of half of the ultimate potential, just to avoid the risk of fumble. Instead, consider capitalizing on the eager competitive spirit of those who are the experts in sale and mass production of your type of product. Think carefully before you choose to delay. AFTER full product rollout, buyers are going to expect proof of ultimate potential, in the form of magnificent sales and stunning profits.

If the time for sale is close to right, and you're close to ready, it simply doesn't pay to wait until every star in the heavens is perfectly aligned. Avoid stress and risk. *Let the wind blow through your hair while you still have some!*

GATHERING MARKET
INTELLIGENCE

One extremely useful element in preparation for sale, which can and should be practiced well in advance of sale, is the gathering of market intelligence. Such intelligence includes data about who the buyers commonly are in your business segment, but it's also much more. It's about how buyers determine value, and what types of companies they like to buy. Discovering long-term trends and patterns in your industry can be immensely helpful when it's time to cash in. Additionally, the accumulation of operating statistical information about others in your industry can be a great tool. It will alert you to problems and opportunities, whether you're considering sale or not. Finally, when the time comes to sell, it gives you powerful ammunition with which to identify and better prove your strengths by comparison to industry norms.

Many business owners think they are gathering intelligent merger/acquisition data simply by dropping into a file the letters of people who write to them with potential interest. First of all, 90% of those letters come from business brokers, investment-fund buyers, and displaced executives who are would-be buyers. These are not the most credible or focused contenders for optimum purchase. Secondly, even letters from viable suitors, who are in the market and who really do know who you are and what you do, are of fleeting value. Buyers who have intent and determination to buy usually make their move within a year or less. Either they get several deals done, after which they are "full" for a time, or they progress further in their study of what they want to buy, and their prime targets evolve.

The process of gathering functionally useful market intelligence is best pursued from several different angles:

1. Who is buying whom, what are they paying for purchase, and what are their long-term strategic targets,

2. What is average and what is good performance in your business niche, and how do you measure in comparison to others in your market, and

3. What are the long-term trends and shifts taking place in your industry, with respect to the basic shape and form of your prime customers, your product, and its delivery?

With respect to the first item—who is acquiring—owners often hear of sale transactions in their industry soon after they happen. However, gathering true information on the details about pricing and other critical elements to the deal may be far more difficult. If you know the buyer or the seller personally—ask. If you don't know them personally but you have the courage to call, or if a chance encounter brings you in touch—ask. Ask what was paid, and what form that payment took. Did they pay with cash, stock, notes payable, or another type of consideration? Was payment made in full at closing, or was some portion of the payment deferred? Did they buy assets only, or did they assume liabilities too? Was the seller required to pay down debt with the proceeds from sale?

Were there multiple bidders for the company? If so, who? Naturally, only the closest of friends or the most distant of acquaintances will answer this wide range of questions openly. However, learn what you can, and take notes. File the information away, because you will someday find it very useful data!

The second bucket of intelligence to gather relates to statistical industry norms. In some industries an owner can gather excellent data of this type directly from trade associations and magazines. More commonly, however, the information which is publicly available is imprecise and not quite on point to the actual business in question. For example, industry categories are often too broad to allow accurate comparisons. Obtain all possible information, but don't use it without careful scrutiny.

Mark Twain said, "There are three kinds of lies: (1) lies, (2) damned lies, and (3) statistics." Statistical comparisons **are** worth the time to obtain and analyze, but only with due care to find information of real pertinence and comparability.

The better segmented and more specific the data, the better. The best information may come from buying groups or joint-venture alliances, or even from conversations with friends. The more you are able to build your understanding of how you fit into the picture of your total market, and where your company is particularly strong or weak, the better you will be able to deal with the questions which will arise in marketing your company.

The third segment of intelligence relates to the big picture. What are the important, sweeping changes coming to your industry segment? The moment you cease glancing up at the horizon to ensure that your direction is true and your progress is steady, you endanger your company's future.

Philip Wrigley, chairman of the great Chicago-based Wrigley Gum Company, was once interviewed by a reporter on a long transatlantic flight. The reporter asked why he traveled tens of thousands of miles every year to personally visit each major market in which the company's product sold. Wrigley quickly replied, "For the same reason the pilot of this plane keeps the engine running when we're already twenty-nine thousand feet up."

It pays to remain vigilant and attentive to changes in your marketplace. If you were an automotive parts warehouse distributor in the 1980s with good future vision, you got out. You realized that this entire layer of the distribution network was heading toward obsolescence.

If you were a conveyor fabricator in the 1990s, you may have seen a great opportunity coming from a veritable explosion in the sophistication of warehouse systems. If you saw and appreciated the changes to come, you may well have begun to develop specialized competency to fit this evolving market. If you did so, you probably doubled your business value very quickly.

In the 1980s, smart automotive parts warehouse distributors sold to the retail chains, which were taking over their entire layer of business function. In the 1990s, conveyor manufacturers combined with system integrators, software designers, and design/build manufacturers focusing on enormous and complex facilities. These were the paths to fast maximization of wealth for such business owners.

The "big picture" elements are the gradual but significant trends. They may be trends for providers to offer a greater range of service. They may be tendencies toward increasing specialization. Unfortunately the more difficult any business is to operate, or the more stressed the operation becomes, the less likely the owner is to distance himself adequately to thoughtfully examine the trends. When business is tough, most owners tend to buckle down and focus on the details with such intensity that they totally lose sight of the big picture.

Some years ago we sold a boat manufacturer owned by a single individual, who was also the CEO. Early in the "getting acquainted" stages, he became completely unavailable for several days while he attended a company planning retreat. Upon his return we asked how the retreat went and if his team was successfully fired up for another good year. He corrected our misconception and explained that he took his planning retreat all alone—just to personally spend time in focus upon where he was and where he was going. He was a tremendously successful business operator, and I'm convinced that his annual retreat helped.

Once every few months the prudent owner will lift his head and try to look from afar. Such vision will offer keen insights not only into prudent operating or marketing direction, but also into sourcing for premium buyers of the future.

PROFITABILITY IMPACT

Is the amount that a buyer will someday pay directly related to company profitability? Yes and no. The amount that the buyer will pay is a direct corollary of two factors:

1) The buyer's estimate of what profit HE will be able to produce by operating your company, and

2) The buyer's perception of the likelihood of competition beating his offer.

Except in cases of newly emerging proprietary technology, the buyer's estimate of profit potential is almost always linked strongly to history. Of that history, clearly the most important element is the most recent time period. Nevertheless, ideally, in preparing for sale, you would like to build a solid and relatively stable historical picture of growth—both in sales and in profitability.

The profit piece of the picture can and always will, from the buyer's viewpoint, take into account ownership quirks. For example, if the owner takes zero salary but works sixty hours per week, the buyer will recognize that a replacement cost will be required, to pay someone else to do the job that the owner is now doing. Alternatively, if the owner works ten hours per week, but pays himself an enormous salary, that salary clearly looks to be, at least in large part, owner return on equity. The buyer will add such salary back to get the true stand-alone profit picture.

Buyers will thus focus upon the "owner–neutralized" historical profits from operations. Buyers also will view the company with an eye to what they believe they can make from it. Thus, if the seller is carrying ten expensive administrative people which the buyer could do without, that will be built into the buyer's analysis. If the buyer thinks he can double sales of the seller in a heartbeat by expanding the seller's product offering to his own existing customer base, that, too, will be a factor.

There is one other peculiarity to this concept of profit impact on pricing that is worthy of mention. Generally, as any market analyst will tell you regarding price-point relationships to earnings, the P/E ratio (price to earnings) doesn't mean anything when there is no "E". However, in the sale of a business as a whole, as a going concern, there are exceptions to this fundamental investment wisdom. Although profitability invariably is a powerful determinant of business pricing, there are situations where even loss operations can produce aggressive competitive pricing among buyers.

We once sold a $30 million plastics company with consistent losses for the past three years running. The company had heavy debt levels, and their banker sponsored a buyer who offered to assume the debts and pay $500,000 for the company. In spite *of the loss environment, we were confident that competition would drive price to at least a few million dollars, and we encouraged the seller to hold on, to resist the pressure from his bankers, and to let us talk with other prospective buyers. In three months' time, the company was sold for $3.5 million in cash. There was no multiple-of-earnings justification and no substantive market value of assets to aid in the value determination. The price came entirely from raw competitive interest.*

Poorly run businesses with low or zero profitability, if they show strong volumes and/or good gross margin, may still be perceived well. If a clear and viable case can be made to buyers that the earnings potential is strong, even where history is weak, buyers will compete for the purchase. Once again though, their appetite and their aggressiveness in pricing will depend on their belief that such competitive pricing is necessary to win the deal.

BUILDING THE SECOND TIER

A company is known by the people it keeps.

The builders of companies are often entrepreneurial geniuses who work very hard in every aspect of their business. They usually find that it's hard to find employees who care as much as they do about the outcome of their business performance. Often they find it easier to keep the ultimate control in their own capable hands, because it is so difficult to develop managers within, able to do an equally skilled job.

As far back as 1720, Voltaire observed, "It's not the scarcity of money, but the scarcity of men and talents, which constrains success." Outstanding people are hard to find.

Buyers want companies with in-house talent adequate to sustain the business, even if the owner, post-sale, decides to retire or work far less. After sale, buyers don't really expect the owner's interest to be as strong as it was before. The owner will no longer be dependent upon the business for his principal personal net worth, as he was before sale.

We see certain traumatic volume thresholds in business development which are standard pressure points resulting from budding needs that come with growth. The talent and capabilities required of second-tier management increase predictably at certain volume thresholds. For example, the $10 million level, and again the $50 million level, seem to be frequent points of trauma.

At around $10 million in volume the owner first comes head to head with the powerful need for a real second-tier management group. The enterprise is simply too large for one owner to do it all by himself. Often the areas most loved by the founding owner are the ones easiest for him to replace first. The natural born engineer will more easily develop great engineering talent than sales skill or human resource talents. The gifted salesman has an innate ability to identify sales talent, and to teach sales management skills. As a result of the often greater ease in developing people in the owner's most natural skill set, the owner often finds himself most easily transitioning away from his strong points. Soon he may be left with greatest responsibility only for those areas that he dislikes. Thus he finds himself working excessively hard, in functions that he finds increasingly unpleasant. Bad combination.

Developing and keeping second-tier talent is a basic need in the quest for achieving value. Test and probe skills, nurture talent, and gradually play out increasing responsibilities to developing management. Seek to ensure that customer relationships are wide and deep, and do not become vested in solitary individuals (including yourself). Establish early policies requiring non-compete agreements for important positions. Look for opportunities to advance people who are good at developing even more talent at the next lower tier. Focus on development for the longer-term future, to prepare for the next wave of growth.

Remember, the only thing worse than training employees and losing them is not training employees and keeping them. Take the time to develop management talent in your organization, and then loosen the reins enough to allow them to flourish.

The more your business is self-sustaining and able to operate profitably and well without your personal time and attention, the better its value will be. Also, the side benefit (not insignificant) is greater personal flexibility for you and greater durability in times of crisis for your company. It pays to work yourself out of a job.

HOUSEKEEPING

In preparing for a successful sale, there is a good deal of house-keeping to consider in advance. Books and records should be cleaned up. Physical plant and equipment should be maintained and renovated. Contractual agreements should be in good form and current. Corporate records should be up to date. The following is a brief checklist of matters to consider well in advance of sale:

Two or more years before sale:

- Write off old assets of questionable value, in one fell swoop.

- Obtain non-competes from key employees.

- Develop a long-term capital equipment plan to ensure no apparent crisis of under-spending just ahead of sale.

- Pay down debt as much as possible.

One year before sale:

- Get clean audited or reviewed financial statements from a qualified CPA.

- Check corporate minutes and shareholder records to be sure all are current and in good form.

- Run a lien check and a Dun and Bradstreet credit report to determine what records others may see about you as they investigate your history.

- Check all patents and copyrights to be sure registrations are up to date.

Three months before sale:

- Clean house physically, at primary operating locations.

- Consider face-lift cosmetics to spruce up physical plant for any trouble spots.

- Consider updated asset and real property appraisals.

Before the buyer's site tour:

- Search inside and outside for anything that might appear to be an environmental or safety hazard; move it, label it, or clean it.

- Make sure all floors are clean, all boxes are neatly and safely stowed, and all workspaces are orderly.

- To the extent practical, dispose of unused supplies, equipment, or inventory; if they can't be eliminated, be sure they're clean, free of dust, and neatly organized.

- Read, clean, and update all bulletin boards and all signage.

- Inform staff that there will be visitors, and request that they continue with work and allow visitors to be impressed; let them know that a pleasant smile is always appreciated.

In a plant tour of a large and very profitable plastics manufacturer, which we represented in sale, the buyer noticed safety statistics on our client's bulletin board. The statistics were, in accordance with OSHA regulations, to have been posted monthly, and yet the most recent report posted on the bulletin board was almost three years old. In fact, every piece of paper on the bulletin board was discolored with age. In the same tour, forklift drivers in the warehouse drove at what seemed to be about 45 miles per hour through the plant. Pallets were stacked high, and in some cases a mid-tier pallet would have cartons slightly caved in, such that the entire tower was tilted precariously. The goods inside were lightweight, but I noticed our touring guests looking up with worried expressions, and walking quickly to move past the threatening towers. The buyer, a large and very safety-conscious company, backed away from the deal because of their concerns.

Consideration of the housekeeping items appropriate to your particular business can save you tremendous headaches in the selling process. Also, and perhaps more importantly, meticulous housekeeping, both with respect to outward appearances and legalistic detail, can do much to enhance the probability of closure. The problem you solve might make the important difference as to whether or not the sale is successfully consummated.

The Selling Process

WHY SELLERS SELL

Most people assume that the vast majority of business owners who sell are probably a little over sixty years old, with no obvious family successor/CEO, and are contemplating retirement. Years of experience have clearly proven to us that this is not the most common profile. There are far more sellers of strong companies who are in their forties. They have been successful and have grown their businesses well, but one day they decide they would prefer to cash in their chips and let someone else take the business onward to its next phase.

Owners become tired of the risk and hassle of business ownership. With each change, and at each new plateau, they face the need for new skills, more people, and improved capital infrastructure.

Often they begin to feel as if their closest partners are the IRS, the DOL, and the EPA. Business owners tend to appreciate Murphy's Law of Business Regulation: *"For every business action there is an equal and opposite government program."* Owners also become intensely frustrated with the raw magnitude of taxes they find themselves paying—usually well over 50%, all in. Because they keep so little of their net profit, they feel that perhaps it just isn't worth it. As one of my clients put it, *"I think I've finally figured out the whole fundamental idea of government. Here it is: if enough people get together and act in concert, they can take your stuff and not pay for it."* Waste in government is, alas, a fact of life, and that too tends to drive business people crazy. *("A billion here, a billion there—pretty soon you're talking real money." Senator Everett Dirkson.)* We have often joked that the tax system is a great boon to our business because of the frustration it creates among business owners. In reality, there is a healthy dose of serious truth to that.

Another element to owner desire for change relates to how a business owner's job function tends to evolve. Often the talents that helped him most in his early years are far distant from the skills required to handle his now more mature company. As a result, he finds himself doing more of what he likes least. This may actually be one of the most intense motivators for sale. Owners are often shy about admitting this as a part of their reason for considering sale, but they shouldn't be. It's a viable and understandable rationale.

Whatever your motives, buyers need to hear, understand, and believe in your reason for sale. If you say, "I no longer have fun in the business, because I have become an administrator, instead of a salesman" (or engineer, or whatever), buyers like that. They think perhaps there is an opportunity for them to do the administrative jobs while you return to your sweet spot—surely a win/win!

If you say, "I've done well but I'm not sure that I have the expertise administratively to take the company to its next level,"

the buyer can understand that. Frankly, most buyers react to
that very positively, because they think they **can** handle the next
leg of growth.

*Several years ago I spoke about private company sales at a
business symposium for middle market owners. The event was
an annual affair and drew a wide range of business types. After
my talk, I was queried by a forty-seven-year-old man who had
been trying to sell his business for almost a year.*

*He explained that he wanted to sell because he was afraid that
his product was going to become obsolete. He manufactured
a patented device used by most of the oil drilling operations
around the world. His market penetration was outstanding,
and yet he worried, because alternative products were consistently being tried in attempts to replace his product at lesser
cost. He told me that this single issue was his most vulnera-
ble point in the courtship of buyers. He asked how I would
suggest he deal with it.*

*I suggested, first of all, that he use his position effectively in
identifying best buyers. He had a proprietary product, which
gave him solid positioning in a market that others would want
to access. Most of the drilling operations worldwide used his
product. If he could identify buyers who longed for entry into
those drilling equipment markets, then even just a few years of
success by his side, with a buyer adding more product offerings,
could be immensely valuable.*

Secondly, I suggested that he consider being absolutely forth-right about his insecurity. Telling a would-be buyer that he had a golden spot or niche, which for years had been much coveted by his competitors, might not be such a bad thing. Admitting that he wasn't able to broaden his product range to fully capitalize on his customer base could actually entice buyers. For the right buyer, this opportunity could provide enough fast value to make the ongoing competitive risk quite palatable.

One year later I did a return guest-speaker spot at the same event. The same business owner was there once again, and he sought me out afterward to thank me and to tell me what a great difference the more direct approach had made in his efforts to sell. He said that in his initial efforts, before last year's seminar, he had met with at least ten buyers and had received no real offers. He went on to say that in the sixty days after our chat, three out of four new buyers he had talked with had made offers to buy his company. He generously gave much credit to our talk for the improvement in his mindset and for his more straightforward discussion approach. He closed a very successful deal, and he was enormously pleased.

There is one final popular and very compelling reason why owners get bold enough to sell. They decide it's time to give more attention to their families and the things that bring them joy in life.

Building a business is a highly absorbing enterprise. It requires tremendous focus, time, and energy, sometimes at the cost of neglect to other areas of our lives. Often after a business owner has spent ten years or more at such effort, he begins to realize that opportunities for certain family and personal pleasures slip away with the passage of time.

Years ago we worked with a client who had decided to sell, because his wife had cancer and he wanted to have more time with her. We got his sale done in about four and a half months, which was excellent under the circumstances, and he went on to have a great time with his wife for almost two more years, before she succumbed to the cancer. I had a discussion with him during a holiday weekend about six months after his wife's death. He told me his wife had been begging him to sell the business for probably five years before he called us. He said that, in retrospect, the memories which the two of them had created in their last two years together would pay greater dividends for the rest of his life than all of his investment of the very large sum of cash he had achieved in sale.

Personal or family needs are an entirely viable reason to contemplate exit from your business.

COMPETITION

When the time comes for a serious move toward sale of your company, **do not** start by giving a smiling nod to the next chance caller inquiring about possible purchase. This is a grave mistake and yet it happens amazingly often. You will not find the optimum buyer by chance. Give yourself at least the possibility of achieving optimal outcome by getting the mechanics of the selling process under control.

Plan the process. Guard confidentiality. Consider potential best buyers carefully. Prepare savory and meticulously accurate information for presentation to buyers. Lastly—and most importantly of all—create COMPETITION.

In order to achieve maximum pricing, there is no single element in the selling process more important than the creation and maintenance of competition. There is a fundamental truth here that every seller needs to appreciate. Competitive pressure always causes buyers to pay more. That is so critical, so fundamental, and so important to success.... Let me repeat it:

COMPETITIVE PRESSURE ALWAYS CAUSES BUYERS TO PAY MORE.

Buyers have a responsibility to buy as economically as possible, regardless of their need or desire for the purchase. They will only pay maximum price if they must, in order to capture the deal. This is the natural law of a free economy at work. Market price governs.

Al Capone once said, "You can get more with a kind word and a gun, than with a kind word alone." Competitive pressure pushes pricing to its maximum.

If the business combination is one of those lovely fits where 1+1=3, who in fact will get the benefit of the "extra" 1? The buyer will not pay that extra benefit to the seller simply to be a nice guy. If the seller isn't courting other competitive suitors at the same time, the astute buyer will perceive that, and will offer only the minimum necessary to secure the deal. The buyer CAN pay more in a 1+1=3 situation, but generally the buyer WILL pay more only if market competition forces him to do so, in order to win the deal.

There is no obligation, just because the buyer can make more money with your business than you can, for him to pay you for that synergy. The buyer will feel that the synergy fairly belongs to him—not you.

Several years ago a prospective client came to us with an offer in hand to buy his company for $10 million. The owner had a feeling that the price was too low, but wasn't sure what his company was worth. We also were uncertain about precise value, but the company was growing tremendously, was extremely well *run, and was in a nice niche which we knew many buyers would be excited about. In this particular instance, the difficulty of the engagement was greatly magnified by the fact that our client preferred to sell to the original prospective buyer, and was reluctant to let others bid. We took the engagement only on the condition that we would be allowed to court alternative buyers, although we still knew full well that our client strongly preferred and hoped to see a deal consummated with the original suitor. We were confident that we could improve price, but were not certain that the original buyer would rise to the occasion.*

Upon accepting the engagement, we immediately made it clear to the buyer that we were talking also to alternative suitors, and that the only way to close the deal without our full-blown courtship of competitive bids was to increase purchase price significantly. In less than thirty days the original buyer increased his proposal from $10 million to $25 million in cash at closing, plus another $15 million in potential additional price, if certain prospective targets were met. The deal closed in sixty days. (Happily, the company has since gone on to exceed every financial target, and both buyer and seller remain pleased.)

Even for a perfect acquisition fit, the buyer will not pay premium price unless absolutely necessary. Competition pushes pricing to the maximum.

INTERMEDIARY SHIELD

Is it necessary, when moving to sell your business, to hire an intermediary, or an investment banking firm, or a business broker? Certainly a business can be sold by the owner directly, but generally it's not prudent.

The skilled intermediary can bring tools and techniques to the negotiating process, which you alone can't access. The professional intermediary will have experience that makes a world of difference. It's like having a machine gun instead of a 22-caliber rifle. The number of techniques at the disposal of the professional will be many times greater, readily at hand, and accessible many times faster, simply because he or she has been there before.

Let's talk specifics. An intermediary can say things about you or your company that simply would not come off as well if said by you directly. *It's like telling a prospective blind date for a friend why she might enjoy the company of your friend. "He's intelligent, he has a great sense of humor, and he's really handsome!" If your friend called the prospective date and said, "I'm intelligent, I have a great sense of humor, and I'm really handsome," it would be far less credible. It simply doesn't work.*

Even the bad news passes through easily with an intermediary. In fact, with the right spin, bad news can actually be used to the seller's advantage. "The owner is a brilliant guy, but quite frankly, he's an engineer. The people side of this business isn't his strength. If you, Buyer, can bring in the people skills needed, this company could soar!" To the buyer with team building as a major strength, this is the perfect fit. The buyer can let the seller remain, doing what he excels at: using his talents to the maximum. The right buyer may literally be likely to triple profitability with minimum additional cost, by fitting his strengths into the precise weaknesses of the seller.

The middleman also gives you the time to think during the course of negotiations. He makes the first foray on all proposals. You get to hear, consider, and strategize about your response before the buyer sees or hears it. You run no risk of knee-jerk frustration, of deal-killing anger, or (at the opposite end of the spectrum) of showing excess glee or relief when a good thing happens. You avoid showing your hand.

When trying to work through a knotty problem, your intermediary can safely float trial balloons. "I have an idea. I'm not sure that my client will go for it, but it seems to me that it could get us most of the way there—if it works for you...."

The intermediary can take the hard stance on an issue and still leave room to back down if necessary. "I'm almost positive this isn't going to work for my client. I will run it by them, if you tell me I must, but I think it makes better sense for us both to try to find some other solution. How would you feel about...."

Any time you inject competition among buyers, an independent professional can help enormously to keep an unbiased tone to the competitive nature of discussions. The owner is not perceived as the hard-nosed "it's–all–about–the–money" bad guy. It's the intermediary's stated job to produce the best and highest offer for the company. He isn't bad for creating a horse race. It's his job.

The intermediary may temper his price focus slightly, but buyers know and understand that he will be and should be safeguarding value. "It's not entirely a pricing issue. Given reasonably close proposals, I know the owner would give up some sales price to do what he feels is best for the people and the company long term. However, that doesn't mean that money is not a factor. It's my job to ensure that the finalists in this process are all at least reasonably close to a solid market value."

Buyers will understand that the owner has a responsibility to his family and/or to other shareholders to cash in reasonably well. If a buyer is within spitting distance on price, it's reasonable for buyers to try to sell their proposal on the basis of non-price intangibles. However, even the world's greatest buyer in terms of the intangibles (culture, attitude, and fit) doesn't expect to get by with offering substantially less than what the company is worth, if there is a professional intermediary involved.

There are also many points along the way where the buyer, too, is happy to have an intermediary sounding board. The buyer may want to make the point that the company's plant is a mess. He would hesitate to tell the seller directly, for fear of insulting him, but perhaps it's seriously bothering him and he's worried about EPA, safety, or other issues as a result. The intermediary gives him a way to lay out his concerns, and to more safely explore what might be done to increase his comfort level about the problem. An experienced and cool third party will hear, understand, and think clearly about creative approaches to explore the problem, and resolve it reasonably.

Lastly, the intermediary usually has more staying power than the owner would in the selling process. The owner has two principal issues that lessen his deal "endurance." (1) The owner has a business to manage. Frankly, if the company doesn't do well on a steady and continuous basis as it approaches sale, all else is for naught. It is very hard to sell a business while paying strong attention at the same time to the running of that business. (2) The owner has a much higher personal, emotional stake in the sale, and his involvement is, accordingly, far more intense and far more exhausting. When a buyer steps back with a "no thanks" after hundreds of hours of courtship, it can be disheartening, and very tempting to give up. The professional intermediary realizes that setbacks are all just part of the game. The professional takes setbacks in stride and quickly retrenches for another approach. The best of the best have amazing tenacity and resiliency.

There is a Chinese proverb that we often quote at my firm: *"The person who says it cannot be done should not interrupt the person doing it."*

All told, there are an enormous number of middleman moves that a smart, independent professional can make most effectively. He must be experienced, highly skilled, and very much in tune with what the owner will want in order to be optimally effective. Those things given, the use of an intermediary can triple the likelihood of eventual success in sale.

SILENCE IS GOLDEN

Everyone has heard the old adage "Protect the goose which lays the golden eggs." In the world of mergers and acquisitions, the goose is the business to be sold. Protecting it means, to a large extent, jealously preserving confidentiality during the selling process.

Most business owners instinctively know this. Customer relationships are critical and, in a competitive environment, may be fragile. If your customers hear that you are considering sale, will they immediately turn to alternative vendors? Probably not, but maybe…and maybe is enough to be dangerous. The larger the business is, the less the sensitivity, but there is always some. Customers worry about key suppliers facing ownership transition. They fear that the people they deal with may change. They fear that the direction or focus of the company may change. They seek not to be dependent upon any vendor, but especially not upon a vendor who may be distracted or disoriented by ownership changes. They seldom abandon a vendor for these reasons, but they certainly might seek to ensure that they have a relationship with an alternative source—just in case.

The second area of exposure to damage from non-confidentiality involves employees. The key people (the best people) in any organization are always desirable in a competitive marketplace. People naturally feel insecure in times of ownership transition. If your people learn that you are considering sale, will they immediately put their resumés on the street? Probably not, but the best ones don't need to. Perhaps they just react a tad differently the next time they are approached by a would-be employer or headhunter. It may be just that little bit of added insecurity about the future that causes them to say, "I really don't know what will happen in the next year. Maybe it is time for me to at least listen to other opportunities."

Even the rank-and-file staff members will be dramatically less efficient with rumor-mill gossip about possible sale as a topic of discussion. It's a tremendously interesting and distracting kind of news. It's an alarming prospect to many. Employee worry and speculation can only harm an employee's productivity and certainly will do nothing to ease the transition post-sale.

In spite of all of these just and reasonable concerns, you simply can't sell a company without telling someone that it's for sale. *It's like winking at a woman (or man) in the dark. If you're the only one who knows what you have in mind, you won't get anywhere.*

How, then, does one protect confidentiality during the selling process? First, the owner should have virtually no conversations with possible buyers without a carefully drawn nondisclosure agreement in place. From the first phone call, there is exposure. The buyer must be made to understand immediately that any conversations must be held in the strictest confidence, and that he is expected to sign a legally binding nondisclosure commitment before any discussions proceed.

Owners often feel that the formal confidentiality agreement is not needed until financial statement details are shared. Not so! The first verbal acknowledgment that you might consider sale at all is a risk and needs to be covered immediately.

We have heard countless stories of the very earliest-stage breaches in confidentiality causing serious problems. The excited potential buyer gets a firm "maybe" from the seller and is enthusiastic. Two hours later he opens a sales meeting with, "Guess who we may be buying?" The damage is done. From there it's a short hop to customers and employees.

The nondisclosure agreement used by our firm identifies the client number, instead of the name. Thus the buyer does not know the identity of the seller until after he signs the nondisclosure agreement. This is clearly the safest route.

Another important benefit to carefully guarding confidentiality comes in enhancement of buyer appetite. When our firm goes through our typical process of selling a company, we do lots of research early on to be sure we have the "right" buyers. As we begin approaching those buyers, we let them know up front that we are careful about selecting only the best-fitting buyers, and that the opportunity will not be presented to a large number of prospects.

This approach does two important things:

- It encourages the buyer to respect and guard the information more carefully, both because the buyer knows it would be easy to trace any confidentiality leak, due to the smaller number of players, and because the buyer PREFERS to keep the deal quiet so that more buyers won't hear about the opportunity and join in the competitive hunt.

- Also, there is an odd sort of psychological impact to keeping the field of buyers narrow. It's more exciting for buyers to know there are fewer contenders. Even though the few we talk with are, we hope, the best and toughest competitive contenders for the deal, buyers still like the opportunity better knowing they are one of a select number of suitors.

If you can't get people to listen any other way, tell them it's confidential. Frighteningly true.

BUYERS—360 °

The majority of business owners who come to us think that they know, at the outset, who their best buyers will be. Ninety percent of the time, they are wrong.

Often the buyer most readily thought of is the head-to-head competitor, who has been there, in competition, for many years. The business owner may also be excited about the longtime suitor who has religiously called every couple of years, for a decade past. The owner quickly jots down his short list, and thinks those are the likely best buyers.

Although the short-list contenders often do want to look, they are rarely, in the end, the most generous buyers.

Direct competitors in many cases can't pay the premium price, because they actually have less to gain. They are already established in similar markets. They know the supply chains. They already compete for the same customers. They may even have a similar distribution network. True, they would always like to knock out a competitor, and they would be a buyer almost certainly at the right price. However, their right price may be a bargain price that the seller never would or should accept.

The overt longtime chaser, who has been calling for years to probe about possible sale, is typically an expert shopper. He keeps his wish list in the file and methodically follows up to try to be at the right place at the right time. To the seller he is the easy solution. Also, because of his steadfast attention, the seller may think he's the one most likely to pay well. After all, he has been calling for years. Alas, though, this buyer is probably a seasoned veteran who will quietly bide his time and buy right or not buy at all. He has all the time in the world and is under no pressure to get your deal done.

So where do the best buyers come from? Oh, what a joy to explore!

My grandma used to say, "Honey, everybody has their own unique set of interests. If we all liked the same thing, the whole world would be after your grandpa."

Buyers come from every direction—a full 360 degrees—and then above and below as well! They may be companies which provide goods or services similar to yours, but who need an adjacent product or service to round out their offering. They may be companies which understand your product well, but who don't yet have an entry to your particular universe of customers. They may be companies which need your geography. They may be companies which are almost like yours, but whose greatest strength matches itself perfectly to your greatest weakness.

Good buyers inevitably pop up in multiple segments. The smart seller methodically investigates all that he can actively ferret out, before deciding whom he will invite to look at his company.

Is that a complicated task? Absolutely. Our firm typically spends hundreds of man-hours just sorting out and exploring our best five to ten categories of buyers, for any single client seller. As intermediaries, it is our job to find out who is buying whom and why. We segment buyers into baskets by likely synergy, or fit. Then we identify perhaps the top ten in each category to call to probe further.

There are some tasks in business that you do knowing full well that 90% of your effort will be wasted. Perhaps only 10% has value. You do the 90% anyway, because FINDING the premium 10% is absolutely worth it. Buyer investigation during the process of selling a business is one of those tasks.

We talk individually to hundreds of potential buyers in a single sale engagement. We ask about their acquisition interests. We ask how important growth is to their business plan, and how likely it is that such growth will occur through acquisition. We ask what businesses they've purchased in the past year. We ask what their rules of thumb are for valuing and pricing the businesses that they buy.

We ask what profitability level they judge to be good performance, and what growth levels they see as desirable and credible. We ask what other key attributes of a business they see as the hot buttons that make an acquisition candidate particularly desirable. We ask what they prefer to avoid in the businesses they buy. We learn everything possible about the buyers' desires and targets.

A few years ago we were in the process of early buyer exploration for a sale engagement, when we encountered two especially eager buyers interested in our client. Both told us that their companies were highly acquisitive and, furthermore, that their personal, individual job success actually was heavily dependent upon getting a number of acquisitions done in the year. Great news! Our favorite kind of buyers! These two suitors ended up pushing the price point to an astounding high. The winner was a hero to his company, and we were heroes to our client. Happy day.

Will buyers actually talk openly about their acquisition needs and interests? Absolutely. There is nothing buyers like better than to be approached by someone with a thorough understanding of what they want, who is able to say, "I have a perfect acquisition candidate for you."

It is far easier for a well-known, bona fide intermediary to ask these questions than it would be for the seller to do so directly. Information would likely be tainted if the prospective buyer knew that he was speaking to the seller directly. However, only the foolish seller would commit to the hundreds of hours necessary to take on a buyer-screening task directly. Always hire professionals. Then make sure they test every angle of fit you can identify. The big win doesn't usually come from the most obvious player.

HONESTY PAYS

It pays, inevitably and invariably, to be forthright in presentation of information about your company to a prospective buyer. Forthright does not mean that you must necessarily share all levels of detail. There may be details that you need to withhold in the interest of protecting confidentiality. For those issues, you simply need to say, "We don't wish to provide that information now." Thus you remain forthright, even when you do refuse to provide information.

With all information that you **are** willing to share, be scrupulously honest. When we take on any engagement, we warn prospective clients that if they aren't comfortable with being forthright, they won't like us. We believe that and live by it— and we are absolutely comfortable that such belief integrates perfectly with a clear profit motive. Superb deals always come from a foundation of truth. Only the most secure buyer will have the courage to push pricing to the maximum. Giving truth **allows** buyers to be bold.

Also, bad news can be far more effectively dealt with in the earlier stages of discussions. To pretend that a problem doesn't exist is a foolhardy deception. Problems are far less important or dangerous when full and fair disclosure is made up front, in a forthright manner. Often the buyer will have no adverse response to the issue whatsoever. In fact, in many cases the buyer will see the problem or weakness as an opportunity for substantive improvement. Particularly in areas where the correction seems relatively easy, the buyer may actually see the potential improvement as low-hanging fruit, or fast and easy money to be made post-closing.

Several years ago we were representing an outstanding equipment manufacturer in sale. The company had a technically superior product and their growth had been strong and steady, despite the absence of any sales force whatsoever. When prospective buyers asked about the company's selling process and people, they explained that virtually all of their growth had been through a constant stream of customers finding them. Unlike our client, competitors in their industry had smooth and polished sales mechanisms to fuel growth. With every buyer, our client was modest, apologetic, and even somewhat embarrassed when the discussion turned to the topic of sales systems. Buyers appreciated such openness about the weakness, and saw opportunity in the solution. Virtually every suitor for the company walked away from the client's shy discussion of this topic with a definite increase in appetite. We sold the company for a superb price.

Buyers of companies control substantial amounts of cash and are generally highly responsible and bright people. (A fool and his money are...a rare combination.) If sale is being considered because of some serious problem pending, the buyer is very likely to ask the right question to unearth the problem.

Furthermore, even if a buyer doesn't unearth the problem in the natural course of events, if it's important, it should be disclosed. Lack of disclosure regarding a material problem will inevitably violate some representation or warranty which will be required in the purchase agreement before the deal is finalized.

If the purchase agreement doesn't explicitly seek information on the specific matter itself, it will, at a minimum, require the seller's representation that he has fairly disclosed any material, potentially adverse matters pending. If you, as a seller, expect to keep the proceeds of sale, you need to have come by them honestly.

THINK BIG

One of the most critical elements to outstanding deal making is the ability to think big. Thinking big doesn't mean just setting a big target price. It means **believing in value**.

Periodically at my firm we have strategy sessions to discuss deal status and to brainstorm about trouble spots. Inevitably one of the most valuable elements of such strategy sessions lies in our ability to help one another build enthusiasm and to redouble our own belief in the worth of our clients. We talk about what it is about each company that has sparkle and sizzle, from varied individual perspectives. Each contributed spark of enthusiasm creates ideas for the team, and nurtures our excitement about the client.

When we have the true, heartfelt conviction that the company we're selling is a wonderful find, it shows. It leaks out in our tone of voice, in our choice of words, and in the gleam in our eye. Our enthusiasm and conviction are contagious to buyers. We aggressively pressure for great prices when we believe that we **deserve** great prices.

Please don't misunderstand this advice. I am not advocating lack of realism. There is a time for everything. Before you begin, look realistically and even skeptically at your position. Think hard. Be tough on yourself. Be realistic about your flaws and risks.

However, when all of that is done, before buyer encounters begin, pause, take a deep breath, and bask in thoughts of your strengths. Build counter-information to deal with problem spots.

Master the art of "psyching up" to a THINK BIG mentality. There is one other tremendous benefit to this mental preparation. Sometimes, thankfully, it happens that buyers exceed our fondest dreams. When that occurs, it is critical to internalize such good fortune and become comfortable with it immediately. The transaction instantly has a new threshold. The business has proven to be worth this lovely new amount. The market has spoken. Raise your sights. Get comfortable quickly with your newly elevated status, and push for continuing improvement with each additional step forward. That is how home runs happen.

EXCLUSIVITY

In order to keep the pressure of competition as tightly drawn as possible, sellers need to avoid entering into an exclusive dealings commitment for as long as possible. Buyers will push for speed. They will submit an agreement for seller acceptance with a tight deadline to pressure the seller into speedy acceptance.

As a client of mine once put it, "I love deadlines. I like the whooshing sound they make as they fly by."

If you have healthy competition, understand that pressure for speed is a sign of sincere interest, but don't be tempted to act rashly.

A smart buyer will always offer a Letter of Intent very early with an exclusive dealings clause, or a "stop-shop." Such a clause requires that the seller agree to cease discussions with alternative buyers. Buyer and seller are thus engaged to be married. As the seller is asked to make this commitment, the buyer in turn makes a pledge at the same time, but usually it's a much less onerous pledge. The buyer, in the Letter of Intent, typically says that he intends to buy the company at X price, and he agrees with all good speed to look into getting the purchase done—for example, to draft documents, complete due diligence investigations, obtain financing, etc. However, the buyer usually may back out at any time if something doesn't work out to his satisfaction.

Obviously this is a fairly one-sided commitment, and thus is a bad deal for the seller. The buyer will argue that it's fair and reasonable, and that it's a necessary concession to make it reasonably safe and economical for him to incur the expense for the next phase of purchase investigation.

In our selling efforts we rarely accept a stop-shop, unless or until the buyer is ready to put down a substantial non-refundable deposit. Buyers don't like that, but they will live with it if they must. Either we work out all of the important terms, get such terms in writing, and mutually commit to go forward (barring fraud or catastrophic events) or the buyer must be willing to move forward without securing our commitment to exclusivity.

Additionally we always make sure that buyers we deal with know that they are not the only ones at the table. As a result, our deals finish more quickly, and with very little backsliding, either in dollar pricing or key terms.

Statistically the vast majority of deals in the United States that progress to the Letter of Intent stage never make it to close. Even for those which do eventually close, all too many may do so only after late-stage price reductions by the buyer. If the seller has narrowed the field down to one buyer, he has little power to fight back when the buyer reduces price. He can either accept the reduction or face the risk and hassle of going back to the market to start over.

When a seller has accepted a deal, and has told alternative buyers that he has done so, he appears to be severely weakened if he then later comes back to say he is available again. Other buyers naturally wonder what went wrong. What did the original buyer learn that made him back out? The seller is in a vastly improved position with alternative suitors if he has not told them of his initial failed attempt.

Some years ago we accepted a Letter of Intent from a buyer, choosing his company over about a dozen alternative suitors. Halfway through his due diligence, this buyer demanded interviews with all management staff. Our client was very sensitive to confidentiality, and interviews with management were clearly prohibited by the Letter of Intent. Without such interviews, however, the bank was going to withdraw financing support, and the buyer would be unable to consummate. We let the buyer withdraw and we took the company back to market, contacting the entire cadre of suitors who had previously submitted bids. Not one of those suitors wanted to re-initiate an offer. They all felt insecure about the fact that we had chosen a buyer, but that the chosen buyer was not now moving forward. We ended up re-marketing the company to all new buyers. In the end we closed at an even better price—but it took us an additional five months of effort and hundreds of hours to find, court, and complete negotiations with the new buyers. A failed transaction can be costly.

In summary—avoid exclusivity for as long as possible. Seek always to court more than one competitive buyer. Keep multiple competitors warm and active, running a side-by-side course until very close to the end, and orchestrate completion to occur quickly after a firm commitment is made.

"ASKING" PRICE

As a company proceeds to market, the first question almost every buyer will ask is, "What does the owner want for the company?" Almost all professional sellers of businesses refuse to set price. Instead, they require the buyer to set his own price.

Buyers will naturally resist going first, if at all possible. It is uncomfortable. If they start too high, they may pay far more than they otherwise would have had to. If they start too low, they may be dismissed as "bottom-fishers," not worthy of talking to.

In spite of the clear strategic advantages to making the buyer set price, sellers are often extremely nervous about refusing to give an "asking" price. They feel rude, or disingenuous, in not being willing to tell a prospective buyer what their expectations are. Furthermore, the buyer may react unhappily or angrily, and exert a great deal of pressure to induce the seller to be more "candid." The seller may be afraid that he will lose a good prospect, and feel almost compelled to throw out a number.

Whoever "starts" the pricing process faces risk. If the seller gives a price, and it is far above the buyer's expectations, the buyer will be annoyed, feeling that the seller is unreasonable and foolish, and the buyer will withdraw. If the seller is lower than anticipated, he will never even know of his error. The buyer will still complain that the price stated is too high. He will moan and fume, and then move forward to get the seller to drop a little more. If he says, "Okay—done," the seller would clearly KNOW that his price was too low. Thus, by stating price, all the seller has achieved is the setting of a solid cap on what he might get for his company.

There is no rule—no ethic—no responsibility **whatsoever** for the seller to preset pricing. Buyers are perfectly capable of competitively venturing price points. Experienced and more sophisticated buyers are quite accustomed to it. They will still need to feel competitive pressure if they are to push the price offered to something near their high end, but they can and will respond.

The payoff for proper handling of the pricing question can be tremendous. We are experienced sellers, having seen pricing on literally hundreds of transactions over the years. Still, we can be and often are surprised. When competition is fierce, it is not uncommon for a few buyers to come in at literally double the pricing of the median on a deal.

The potential cost of error in this area is simply too enormous to dismiss. It pays to hang tough and **make** the buyer set the price.

THE RIGHT RESOURCES: INTERMEDIARIES

In selling a company, it is absolutely critical, if you are to maximize results, to get the right team of resources working for you. The team here includes the intermediary who will represent you overall, the attorney who will handle document negotiations, the CPA who will coach your team on the tax aspects of the transaction, and the internal resources who will support the gathering of necessary information and may even be involved in late-stage interviews with prospective buyers.

The intermediary will be the one who finds your buyers, who makes the initial approaches to these buyers, who responds to buyer inquiries and proposals, and who ushers the entire process along to fruition. It's a critical job. This person will make the most—or the least—of your life's work. It's a scary thing to consider handing over such immense responsibility to someone you hardly know.

If you don't give this task to someone specifically skilled and practiced in this very thing, you are absolutely guaranteed to achieve lesser results. Neither your attorney, nor your CPA, nor your COO, nor your lifelong smart businessperson pal will even come close to the capabilities of a well-qualified professional. A professional firm will spend hundreds of hours focused upon this one task for you. It is their job. They won't be interrupted by a separate workload to distract them, and they won't be losing a client when they successfully complete your sale. They exist to sell companies. This job is far too important to place in the hands of someone for whom it's a sideline. You deserve to be the main event.

Normally, business intermediaries will not be people you know and have worked with before. If all they do is sell businesses, you probably have not needed their services before. So how do you know they are good?

Begin with selecting a firm that focuses entirely upon buy-and-sell transactions. There are hundreds of consultants and assorted business advisors who have some experience, but who do other things as well. They will not be as competent, as well staffed, or as experienced as the specialist.

You need an intermediary whose fundamental **livelihood** depends upon successful closings. If your deal is only supplemental income to a separate core business, it will not receive the same intense dedication. *It's a little like bacon and eggs. The hens are involved, but the pigs are committed.*

Check references. It's necessary and prudent to check that they have, in fact, done a competent job for other business sellers. An intermediary's clients were themselves business owners cashing in on a life's work, just like you. They will usually talk with honesty and forthrightness to the reference contacts that call them.

It is worth the time and trouble to make those phone calls. I'm often amazed to be hired by business owners who haven't spoken to any of our references. Although we're naturally honored to have such trust, this seems incredibly dangerous to me.

As you study an intermediary's proposed fee schedule, it is also important to seek someone who will design a strong incentive system that you like. There is no better insurance for keeping someone aggressively working on your side than to be sure they are paid very well if, and only if, they succeed for you.

A part of your selection decision will be, and should be, dependent upon your personal chemistry with the lead person or people. Be sure that you get acquainted with the key people who will be personally handling your transaction. You will be depending upon them for a very important job. You must be able to make your needs and wishes clearly known to them, and you must be able to understand their communications back to you.

Lastly, always ask about success rates for any intermediary you consider. Although no one will be 100% successful, the best can come pretty close.

THE RIGHT RESOURCES: LEGAL COUNSEL

In a sale transaction, the legal representation you need will likely involve a lead attorney different from the key person with whom you have historically worked. You need an expert, experienced and seasoned in business sale transactions. You need a specialist. From a technical standpoint, your legal counsel will play a critical role, and you will depend on him in important ways to monitor and control the purchase agreement. The average purchase agreement is fifty to one hundred pages long, plus exhibits and attachments. It's a complex and formidable document, and your attorney is your bodyguard.

A doctor, an engineer, and a lawyer were arguing over whose profession was the oldest. "On the sixth day, God took one of Adam's ribs and created Eve," said the doctor. "So that makes him a surgeon first." "Please," said the engineer. "Before that, God created the world from chaos and confusion, so he was first an engineer." "Interesting," said the lawyer smugly, "but who do you think created the chaos and confusion?"

I once had a client who expressed very clearly the normal business-owner reaction to those horribly complex legal contracts. He said, *"Trying to understand this contract is like trying to follow a plot in a bowl of alphabet soup."*

In spite of the complexity and the dangers, when choosing the attorney to guide you through this morass, you need to look for more than technical genius and protective instinct. To succeed, you must also screen for the ability to compromise creatively. You want someone who closes deals—not someone who "saves" his client from every good buyer who comes close. The best are those attorneys who focus on getting the desired deal done, and who can consistently keep their egos in check. Ask about track record. Find out how many deals they have worked on in the past year, and how many have closed, and how many have failed.

Ask prospective attorneys to talk you through what makes them successful. Check references. Look for abilities to compromise and understand the opposing view. Value tenacity, but try to make sure it's tempered with calmness and with creative problem-solving capabilities. If the focus of their discussion is to boast about their "saves" which didn't get to closing, go on to the next candidate.

The best deal attorney I have ever worked with was a low-keyed, even-tempered technical genius, who was virtually impossible to anger. In spite of his doggedly courteous and mild-mannered approach to the other side, he was incredibly tenacious. He invariably knew the documents cold, and came back gently but ever so repeatedly with various alternative approaches to winning his each and every point. When he reached an impasse, he didn't mislead the opposition by acquiescing, but he would back gently off for the moment, saying, "I'm not sure I'm comfortable with that. Perhaps if we move on for now and leave that issue alone, we'll come to some alternative which can work a little later." By the sixth pass on the same issue, his methodology was apparent, and yet it was still hard to circumvent. Eventually he won eight out of ten points, and he always prevailed on the important ones. Just as importantly, he never, in all of my experience with him, killed a deal.

The great ones never kill the deal. They find creative solutions that minimize risk to their client, but still get the job done. In the end, they always come back to the client with sensible and pragmatic advice about risk and reward.

Deal-killer attorneys quickly draw lines in the sand. They are fast to offer advice that "everyone does it this way," with the corollary implication that "anything less would be outrageously unfair." Everyone does not do it ANY way. The "always require this" approach is deadly. In mergers and acquisitions there truly are norms and mores, but there is no hard-line standard. Every problem has a variety of reasonable solutions if the parties are industrious enough and creative enough to find them.

THE RIGHT RESOURCES: CPAs

CPAs have a set of problems and issues in a sale engagement different from other advisors. Your CPA will, in all probability, lose ongoing annuity revenue when and if you are successfully sold, because the buyer will later switch to his own CPA. You will use your normal CPA for the deal, and you will need his involvement. He will feel that his job is to help and protect you. However, you need to take his advice carefully. Make it clear to him that you do want to achieve sale. If you have a deal that you want to accept, make sure he understands that this is your goal.

I grew up as a CPA. I was an audit partner with one of the then Big Eight CPA firms and spent sixteen years in the practice of public accounting. CPAs are taught early in their careers that their job is to become a hero by saving clients from bad things. When CPAs find themselves in transaction analysis, they gravitate very quickly to the search for hidden evils.

I ran a multi-functional merger and acquisition group for my CPA firm, working with audit, tax, and consulting professionals in various merger and acquisition transactions for clients around the Midwest. Very often we found our professionals "saving" clients from things that our clients did not want to be saved from.

*I once was involved in a $300 million deal that was very near-
ly killed by a $20,000 tax exposure. The deal was about $70
million better than others that had been proposed, and our
client was thrilled. One of our young tax men kept warning of
an issue that he was concerned about, and predicting tax doom
to come, as a potential result of this issue. Our client naturally relied on the firm to help him ferret out tax exposures, and
was accordingly very worried. Finally, we sat down and under-
took the task of defining what the real dollar exposure was for
this tax problem. It was $20,000. Tops. We found out in time
to avoid harm, but it was embarrassing.*

In my experience as an intermediary, one in four of the CPAs
representing our clients has been supportive and highly effective, protecting the client, but consistently keeping the client's
end-game objective in mind. Another one in four of the CPAs
we have worked with has gone to the other extreme—being
absolutely obstructive to any transaction. They obstruct in part
because they fear losing a client, but even more importantly
because they are generally fearful and mistrusting of any transaction. Often they can't imagine why their client could possi-
bly want to consider sale in the first place. They imagine that
their clients "have it made" because they're earning strong
profits. They simply do not understand the sense of risk a business owner often feels. The remaining population of CPAs is
typically neutral to slightly resistant, mostly in the name of
protectionism.

The right way to get optimal accounting help and advice is to
talk to your CPA openly and honestly as the transaction moves

forward. Be crystal clear in making your desires and objectives known to your CPA, stressing that you want to save tax dollars, you want to understand risks, but you want, in the end, to accomplish sale if at all possible. Also, you might consider a nice bonus to your CPA at closing, for a job well done. He is losing a client, and he does have to be a bit selfless to help you to get the job done. Recognize and appreciate that fact, be straight with him in communications, and he will probably try very hard to do the right thing.

THE RIGHT RESOURCES:
INTERNAL

During the course of sale you will need to accumulate fairly substantial information. Obviously you will need financial statements, which are probably already in hand, but you will need a great deal more as well. There will be questions about financial details and about accounting methodologies. Buyers will want to understand customer concentrations. They will want to understand your markets, trends, and competition. They will want to understand geographic mix, product category mix, mix by salesman or rep, and a wide range of factors relating to the overall revenue environment. They will want to see organizational charts, background on key second-tier management, payroll cost information, and more. They will want data on equipment and facilities and taxes and legal status, and the list goes on.

Much of this data is awkward for an owner to obtain without some internal collaboration, at least with a key financial person. Accordingly, some level of involvement for certain staff may be absolutely necessary.

The owner's primary job during the selling process should be to continue to run the operation well. That may be extremely hard to do with a highly hands-on role in the gathering of information for buyers. Thus extensive owner participation in the information gathering process is probably misspent time.

Often a financial helper can be enlisted without full disclosure of the selling process being contemplated. Many owners gather data for the initial phases of the process, explaining that they are exploring value for estate planning or financial planning purposes, and simply avoid any more detailed explanation to assisting staff. Some owners have their CPAs gather data, although that, too, typically requires some explanation, because the operational information required is generally well beyond the scope of standard audit or tax procedures.

Regardless of the assistance you may need from supporting staff, you will be well advised to keep shared information about the possible sale to a minimum. *I have never met a seller in twenty years who regretted secrecy in the matter of contemplated sale. However, I have met many who regretted sharing too much information.* Be guarded and move slowly in communi cations with staff.

PROCESS TIMING

The total process of selling a business can take anywhere from two months to two years. Two months is unusual in the extreme, and requires aggressive buyers in hand at the outset and a willingness on the part of the seller to settle for nominal investigation of possible competitive bidders. On the flip side, two years is extremely slow, and generally would indicate a serious problem.

A reasonable aggregate timeline would be six to ten months. The first two to three months are generally required to gather information about the company for presentation to buyers and, at the same time, to identify and research who the best buyers may be.

Information to be presented needn't be pulled to an elaborate bound-book format in this process. In fact, we recommend strongly against any printed material which cannot be easily updated and revised as the process evolves. However, material does need to be accurate, professional, and presented in a way to clearly set forth key elements to the deal which make the opportunity attractive to buyers. The package of data which you give to buyers is a selling piece, albeit very soft sell.

With respect to buyer search work, the temptation to rely on old biases and assumptions about possible buyers makes it difficult for anyone heavily involved in the company to gain adequate distance to think most creatively. Also, the time to do a quality job in buyer search is extensive. Hired help is worthwhile.

After information is well developed and you are ready to launch, the early contact stage can be expected to take about another two months. For any given buyer prospect, it may take anywhere from one day to ten days just to get the confidentiality agreement signed, depending on whether or not the buyer requires advance legal review before signing. The longer and more complex your confidentiality agreement, the longer the timeline will be. Although our firm generally uses a very straightforward one-page document for this, we have at times had to deal with longer formats, due to a client's attorney preference.

On one engagement we had a confidentiality agreement which was a four-page, difficult-to-read document which our side's counsel required of all buyers. In spite of the fact that it really wasn't substantively tougher than others and didn't require anything unreasonable or onerous, it inevitably went to the buyers' counsels before they would sign. It took every buyer at least two weeks to return the thing to us with first comments. Then we spent a week or two in almost every case negotiating the confidentiality terms in advance of even beginning to talk about our client. A full month was added to our timeline.

The nondisclosure agreement needs to say that all information, verbal or written, is to be held as confidential. It needs to say that buyer contact to the offices of the company is prohibited. It needs to stipulate that the very fact that the owners are considering the possibility of sale is confidential. If going to a specific and critical competitor, information may need to be limited to named top people only. The agreement should provide for return or destruction of all information on the company at the seller's request. Generally, even the longest and most horrific nondisclosure agreement will focus principally on these major items. If it's possible to say it simply, do yourself a favor and do so.

From signing of the confidentiality agreement it will typically take several more weeks to get the buyer the first phase of information, and for the buyer to consider their initial interest level. The faster that buyers return to you with eager requests for further data, the better. Detailed questions are a good sign of real interest.

By the time you get to the stage of explicit response to buyer questions, you're likely to be at the three- or four-month mark. When you have a nice mix of interested parties and you have provided them with solid information, it is time to call for bids. Best buyers should, by this time, be fairly far along in their thinking and able to establish price quickly. Bids can generally be requested with as little as a week's notice, if all is in place.

When bids are received, it is prudent to select more than one party to continue discussions with. Next-phase actions will include invitations for tours of facilities, and meetings with the CEO or owner. Arranging such visits will probably take several more weeks, but, if all goes well, you will then be set to enter into a Letter of Intent with your chosen favorite, or move directly toward the Definitive Purchase Agreement.

It shouldn't take more than a few weeks to negotiate the formal Definitive Purchase Agreement, and not more than another sixty-ninety days to complete due diligence and close. Save all possible time by encouraging buyers to progress on due diligence, financing, and any other matters, even as you complete the negotiations. If there's a problem or a hitch, it's better for everyone to face it as soon as possible, and either resolve it or move on.

Regarding timing, keep in mind that faster is ALWAYS better. A hundred things can go wrong and foil the sale. A handful of things WILL go wrong—inevitably. They have to be fixed, and fixed, and fixed again to stay on track. The tighter the timeframe, the less opportunity for fate to introduce all new and not all fun challenges to your successful completion of sale.

LETTER OF INTENT

As the buyer hones in on a price point in a business purchase, he often moves rapidly toward formalizing his proposal in a Letter of Intent. Professional intermediaries working for a seller often request something similar in the early stages of price point discussion, but they will call it a Letter of Interest.

What's the difference? The Letter of Interest stipulates a bid on the company, with principal terms outlined, and with price point specified, but it is typically nonbinding. The Letter of Intent, on the other hand, often includes the above outline of terms and price, but also requires an exclusivity commitment on the part of the seller, provided that he accepts. This means that the seller agrees to be legally obligated to cease any discussions about possible sale with alternative buyers.

In either the Letter of Interest or the Letter of Intent, the transaction will still be subject to due diligence on the part of the buyer, and usually will be subject also to the buyer obtaining necessary financing, lender and board of director approvals, and more. All of these are open, easily manipulated mechanisms for the buyer to back away from the deal if he chooses to. If the buyer does not wish to go through with the purchase, it is very easy for him to let the bank know of his preference, and I guarantee you that the bank will then be happy to deny his loan. Accordingly, the seller should never be fooled with a false sense of security that the deal is substantially done at the point of Letter of Interest or Letter of Intent.

One way to ensure that the buyer is making a bona fide commitment to the purchase is to require a nonrefundable deposit. The deposit will be difficult to protect for the seller, because a buyer will naturally want certain qualifications to any possible forfeiture, which is entirely reasonable. For example, the buyer will not allow the deposit to be forfeited if the seller backs out. The buyer will want protection in the event of having relied on false or fraudulent information provided by the seller. The buyer will want some ability to recoup his deposit in the event of a material adverse event, such as the building burning down.

In order to make the Letter of Intent reasonably strong and potentially binding enough to require forfeiture of a deposit, all of the sensitive details remaining in the negotiations will need to be hashed through and agreed to by the parties, in advance of signing the Letter of Intent. Often when the parties have gone that far, it's almost as easy to go directly to Definitive Purchase Agreement, bypassing the Letter of Intent stage altogether.

For those who need or want a Letter of Intent stage in the process, a few comments are in order. I have seen Letters of Intent which were so vague and so difficult to interpret that they were virtually worthless, except to the benefit of the buyer in that the seller is now poised for risk of legal damages if he backs away from the deal. The following comments highlight just a few of the most common and most glaring flaws often presented at the Letter of Intent stage, along with suggestions for how to cope.

Unclear pricing:

Many early-stage letters will include a price range instead of an actual, firm price. Why, if a buyer has won the seller's consent to proceed with a "price range" presentation, would any buyer ever settle upon anything greater than the minimum price stipulated in the range? (Ranges are OK for a Letter of Interest, where no seller commitment is yet required, but are not acceptable for a Letter of Intent.)

Often initial price forays make it unclear what exactly is to be purchased. There can be a tremendous difference if the price is only for gross assets, or if the price includes all assets and acceptance of responsibility for all liabilities. There can also be a tremendous tax impact for a stock sale (federal capital gains rate of 20%) versus an asset sale (more ordinary income, and likely double taxation—often aggregate rates of 45% plus). Make sure you have a clear, written definition of what the proposal entails in terms of format (stock or assets), and in terms of specific assets or liabilities to be included.

Are there assets in multiple entities, such as real estate owned separately? Does the proposal include purchase of cash on hand, and does the seller have the right to remove or pay out portions of such cash before closing? What happens to earnings between the date of the Letter of Intent and closing? (The seller still owns the company, and still has the risk of operating it, so he may well expect that a price adjustment to recoup interim profits is reasonable.)

Until these matters are clearly resolved, you really cannot make an intelligent assessment of the deal being proposed.

Confidentiality restrictions during due diligence:

The buyer will often expect open access to information between the date of signing of the Letter of Intent and the closing date. However, there may be a number of possible restrictions to such access which are entirely reasonable and necessary as protection of the seller. Buyers may wish to contact customers to see that they're satisfied. This is tremendously dangerous. You can never be certain that the deal is truly going to close until the cash is in the bank. If the buyer is a competitor, he may use the due diligence opportunity to learn valuable competitive information about your customer relationships, or even to court your customer for later follow-up.

Buyers may wish to interview employees. This, too, is perilous. If the employee doesn't like the buyer, he may leave. If the buyer doesn't like the employee, the employee may sense that, and try to derail the deal. In that case the owner, in effect, has given his employees veto right over his sale.

Buyers may want their auditors, EPA consultants, insurance advisors, and others to have access to records during working

hours. It is extremely difficult to keep multiple outside professionals adequately sensitized to confidentiality as they spend
time and chat with employees.

All of these issues are solvable. Outsiders can sign explicit confidentiality agreements, and can work as if they're doing a project for current ownership. Customers can be surveyed regarding satisfaction, with a silent listener from the buyer's management group. Employees can be introduced to buyer staff in the
guise of planning, or sales or joint venture considerations.
Highly sensitive matters can be deferred until the very last
moment before closing, so that if the deal fails, corrective
action can be taken very quickly, and interested parties quickly
informed that the deal is off.

The buyer's need for information is real, but so are the seller's
concerns. Chances for successful closure will be dramatically
enhanced if buyer and seller talk reasonably through the issues
in advance, and settle upon livable solutions.

Timelines for completion:

In the first draft of a Letter of Intent the buyer will generally try
to provide for as much time as possible to close, in order to
allow maximum cushion. Typically the letter will provide for
closing in 90 to 120 days. I have even seen letters with proposals as far distant as six months or even a year. Ridiculous!
If the seller has received strong preliminary data and understands the company, and if decent financial information is available and records are in reasonably good shape, many deals can

go all the way to closing in sixty days. If there are no complicated or time-consuming steps involved (i.e., no EPA review
requirements or outside appraisals to obtain), and if the seller
doesn't need additional financing to complete the deal, the
timeline can sometimes be as rapid as thirty days.

Buyers want long timelines generally because they don't want
the risk of having spent significant time and money to get the
deal done, with failure at the end simply because the clock runs
out. Also, in spite of the fact that you may have signed an
exclusive dealings commitment, the buyer still worries that
some random alternative buyer will call you out of the blue and
make you an offer you would love to accept. These are rational worries, and deserve respect in the negotiation. Nonetheless,
you do, inevitably, increase risk of transaction failure by allowing a long timeline.

Consider multiple timelines to benchmark progress. The exclusivity commitment might be void if you can't agree on the
Definitive Purchase Agreement within thirty days. All financial
due diligence might be required to be complete within forty-
five days. Walk through key steps to completion, identify the
critical landmarks, and define requirements for the Letter of
Intent to remain in force. While the buyer is spending money
for legal counsel and for advisors to complete due diligence,
you know he is sincere. When progress stops, your deal is
probably in trouble, and the sooner thereafter that you can be
free, the better.

DEFINITIVE PURCHASE AGREEMENT

The Definitive Purchase Agreement (commonly shortened to "the Definitive" by those of us who know it and love it) is the binding and conclusive agreement to detailed terms for sale of the company. It is a forbidding, exhausting, long compilation of complex legal language. This is where your team of brilliant attorneys will become critical.

Briefing readers on all of the intricacies of the issues pertinent here would be impractical, but I do want to alert you to a few of the principal trouble spots most often misunderstood by sellers.

Structure and terms:

I am frequently amazed at the lack of clarity documents may provide about fundamental structure and terms. You, as a normal business person reviewing the document, should be able to clearly ascertain how much is being paid, and what is being purchased. You should understand any mechanisms for post-closing adjustment, after a closing date audit is complete, and you should understand how any additional price paid or refund of price paid will be handled.

If there are deferred payments, such as notes to be paid over time by the buyer, consider carefully their collectability. I would always opt for cash over any deferred payment, even if it means quite a bit less in price. It is hard to protect against non-collection risk. If the cash up front isn't enough to induce you to sell, think twice (no—more than twice) before you count on deferred payments. If you must allow deferred payments, protect them aggressively. If the buyer is corporate, they will likely form a shell acquisition corporation to do the deal. Make the parent company guarantee. If the buyer is an individual, require personal guarantees. Furthermore, if the spouse doesn't sign too, that personal guarantee may be virtually worthless when it's time to collect. Get a second deed of trust on a home. Get a deep-pocketed relative's guarantee. Beef up every possible protection, or don't count on getting the deferred payments.

If there are payments contingent upon future performance, be meticulous in how you define the performance bogies. Performance targets can be made impossible to achieve by a buyer imposing heavy intercompany or administrative charges, by changes in accounting methods, or by many other diversions of sales or profits. The simpler and more easily defined the targets, the more likely you can avoid later dispute, and thus protect your rights.

My strong suggestion in all of the issues relative to fundamental pricing and terms is to make sure your CPA or other astute financial advisors also review this document. If there are discrepancies or confusing issues, insist on reworking them until all questions are clearly eliminated.

Representations, warranties, and indemnifications:

Every seller will be asked to make representations and warranties about the company he is about to sell. He will be asked
to rep that he has been honest and truthful. Easy. However, he
will also be asked to rep that nothing has occurred under his
reign which will impair the future assets or performance of the
company. Furthermore, he will be asked to promise to indem-
nify the buyer if some foul surprise from the past later pops up.
Not so easy.

Keep in mind that if the buyer does not ask you for a pretty
aggressive set of reps and warranties, something is wrong. If
the buyer is paying an aggressive price for the company, he naturally will want your promise that he is getting exactly what
you told him he's getting. If he asks for nothing, you should be
worried, because it probably means he's getting a bargain.

Most sellers are comfortable making reps and warranties about
things they know about. Honesty and full disclosure should not
be issues. Correct reporting of liabilities can be ascertained by
CPAs. Taxes for the period of ownership can't be escaped in
any case, so if later tax audits expose problems for the period
prior to closing, it's no more burden than the owner already had.

However, owners become very nervous about things that may
have occurred on their watch, but which they may not know
about. Your professional negotiators should limit all possible
reps and warranties to "the best of seller's knowledge." There
should be a ceiling on aggregate possible exposure to any sell-

er indemnifications post-sale. There should be a threshold to prohibit multiple small dollar claims, with some sort of diminimus rule. If there is a truly critical exposure point, both buyer and seller might consider insurance to provide protection. This is a complex set of issues, but one worth patience and tenacity to achieve a balanced and reasonable outcome. When all is said and done, risk to the seller should be managed and limited, and should be nominal to the aggregate outcome, or the seller shouldn't do the deal.

Ancillary agreements:

There will probably be multiple ancillary agreements, such as employment agreements, noncompetes, leases, and more. Although ancillary, these are not unimportant elements to the transaction.

Employment agreements generally are much more easily enforced against the employer than the employee. Nonetheless, they should be established under bona fide terms, which the seller can live with prospectively. Sometimes buyers like to divert part of the purchase price to an employment contract, in order to make payments tax deductible. However, if the agreement calls for full-time employment, even if the buyer says that real full-time work will actually not be necessary, the seller should ascertain that he is truly comfortable living with the exact written terms of the agreement before he signs.

Most sellers are happier in the end with a relatively short-term employment agreement, even if they think they will likely pre-

fer to stay longer.   Until you and the new buyer live together
for a while, it is very difficult to predict how much you will like
the new working environment.

We have had sellers who thought they wanted to work for many
years, who decided within three months that they would be
gone tomorrow if they could. On the other hand, we have had
sellers who wanted to be gone tomorrow, who later found that
they were, to their surprise, having more fun than ever before.
(Sometimes having the parent corporation perform all of the
administrative functions and worry about financing growth can
make running a company a lot more fun.) In either case, the
requirement to renegotiate, if a longer-term relationship is
desirable, tends to make both sides to the deal behave more
nicely toward one another post-sale. It also gives the seller the
clear freedom to do other things if it's not working.

Noncompete agreements will always be required in connection
with sale, and are reasonable and necessary. However, sellers
should make sure that the agreement they sign is sensibly limited to areas of business their company is in at the date of sale,
and isn't allowed to spill over to whatever new venue their
buyer may choose to get into in the future. A reasonable time
period for a noncompete is generally two or three years,
although I've seen some as brief as one year, and a few as long
as five. The date of inception of the noncompete is also important. Most buyers will require that the noncompete continue in
effect for at least some time after employment ends. Sellers
should be cognizant of the issue, and watch the effective dates.

The Definitive is the guts of your final sale agreement, and is worth time and torment to understand and protect, in spite of the complexity and length (usually one hundred or more pages, including exhibits). We often read as many as ten or more versions of the Definitive from start to finish in the course of one deal, with changes to every single page. Negotiation of the final agreement takes hundreds of hours, and may be as much as a third of the total time spent in getting the sale done. This is where those great professionals you have on your team should shine, and you deserve and should expect at least a couple of thorough sessions to explain and strategize about the issues.

Negotiating Techniques

THE VALUE OF RAPPORT

There is a tremendous advantage to establishing a heartfelt, sincere, like-each-other rapport with the other side to the transaction. Every element of the negotiation will proceed more smoothly with a pleasant relationship at the foundation. There are two powerful keys to establishing such a personal rapport.

The first is to make a sincere effort to get to know the other party, and to cause them to feel that they know you. When we know that someone has values similar to ours, family issues familiar to us, or other core commonalities, we naturally tend to feel that we understand them slightly better. We have a natural desire to please and get along with people that we understand, and people that we deem to be "friends."

Remember to be respectful and courteous toward the other person's personal religious, political, or ethnic views, even when they are vastly different from your own. If you can't keep your mind open, keep your mouth shut, too.

My firm was once representing a buyer in the search for a specific niche manufacturer. After exhaustive research, we found the perfect company, based in rural Arkansas, and owned by a staunchly religious Southern Baptist family. In getting acquainted with the prospective seller, we learned that (a) he didn't drink, gamble, smoke, dance, or play cards, (b) he lived in a dry county and was proud to tell us that most of the local employees were of similar conservative background, (c) he leaned to the extreme right politically, and (d) he felt that the character of the possible buyer might well be more important to him in sale than any other factor—including price. We communicated all of this very explicitly to our somewhat wild and woolly New York client, and after about forty hours of patient discussions with the seller, we were finally able to arrange a meeting. We flew and drove for a long trip to arrive at the seller's place of business late in the day. The buyer sent his son from their Los Angeles plant to represent him at the meeting. The son showed up in an "Elton John Aids Benefit" T-shirt, with long hair and a ponytail, carrying a huge Santa-style mesh bag of beer-logo cups as a gift for our seller friends. The deal was literally dead before we even got inside the door.

Although you don't need to share the other party's perspectives or philosophies, you do need to be sincerely respectful of their viewpoint, at minimum.

The second key to building personal rapport is laughter. It's amazingly hard to dislike someone whom you laugh with. It's also amazingly hard to get seriously tough in negotiations with such a third party.

Legendary baseball great Dizzy Dean was once up to bat, and reacting to a called strike, he shouted at the umpire, "You jerk, that ball was a mile high!" The ump scowled at Dizzy, shook his head, and said, "Come off it, Dizzy, that ball was coming so fast you didn't even see it." Dizzy understood the potential penalty of a hostile, angry ump calling those pitches for the rest of the game, and he thought fast. He shuffled his feet a little, kicked at the bat, and looked like a sulky kid, while he mumbled, "Well, it sure sounded high." The ump laughed, and couldn't help but like Dizzy just a little bit more for the rest of the game.

Those who laugh with us naturally find it difficult to feel antagonistic or hostile toward us.

F. Lee Bailey, one of the most notorious and successful defense attorneys of all time, has a famous bit of wisdom, which he has often shared with younger attorneys. Mr. Bailey says, "Laughing jurors don't convict." He has proven it literally hundreds of times. One recent example may be the O. J. Simpson case. F. Lee Bailey was the original senior attorney on that case. Is it a coincidence that Johnny Cochran dotted his defense strategy with little bursts of thinly disguised play? Was it pure personal whimsy to compose little rap-like ditties for his defense remarks? Probably not. "If it don't fit, you must acquit!" Jurors laughed. They couldn't help but find Cochran amusing in a warm and playful way. True to the traditional F. Lee Bailey advice, those jurors did not convict.

PLAYING HARD TO GET

In the business of selling businesses, we tease about the need to give remedial lessons to our male staff members in "playing hard to get." Such gamesmanship truly does have a place in the sophisticated world of mergers and acquisitions.

An eager buyer, who believes competitors will want the target company, will pay more. He will pay faster. He will be less squeamish about fine points and details of the negotiated terms that don't go his way. The last thing in the world he wants is to enable his competitor to get a foot into the door of "his" deal, simply because he was a little too slow or he tried a little too hard to get a bargain. He will even, if necessary, pay a premium price to prevent competitive intrusion.

Thus it pays to be sensitive to the details that cause buyers to feel the heat of competition. If you, as the seller, call every few days to check on the status of the deal, will that whet the buyer's appetite? Of course not! If you do that, he will see that you are chasing.

Take a lesson from your adorable sixteen-year-old daughter. The phone rings; she glances at the caller ID, smiles, and says, "Tell him I'm not home, please, Dad." Dad hangs up the phone; she smiles, tosses her head, and says, "Thanks." This girl will never be the chaser, and the boys know it. It only makes them want her more.

Take a lesson from professional athletes. Look at what happened to their compensation with the advent of free-agent status.

The seller who is pursued by multiple buyers is much different from the seller who must chase buyers. Buyers will view the two entirely differently. If the seller initiates each step in the chase, the buyer will assume that there aren't many alternative suitors out there. If there were others, surely this seller would not seem so desperate.

The prudent seller remains cool enough to let the buyer chase him. Answer questions and be responsive, but do not chase.

MIRRORING

One of the greatest people techniques in the world, with almost universal applicability, is something psychologists refer to as "mirroring." Basically, mirroring involves matching another person's style or mood, in order to establish a better connection. It's a magnificent technique helpful in negotiating, in selling, and even in general human relationships—business or personal. It works amazingly well!

It's hard to appreciate how extraordinarily effective mirroring is unless you try it. The simplest, fastest way to get acquainted with mirroring might be to try it the next time you come home to a depressed or sad spouse or sweetheart. Oftentimes our natural tendency in that circumstance is to help them out of the mood with a smiling "cheer up, honeybun!" We smile brightly, and try to maintain our sunniest possible disposition in order to pull them up.

The next time, try instead to go down and join them in their misery. Empathize with their woes, and chime in with your own as well. Wallow with them in abject despondency. Within thirty minutes (sometimes within five), you'll find them starting to perk up. They clearly feel better. Is it because they wanted you sad also? Of course not! It's simply human nature to feel more connected with someone on our own wavelength. It is a fact of our basic humanity that such connection with another person (especially someone we love and trust) makes us feel better. Pretty soon you'll find them cheering you up with jokes and lighthearted suggestions for fun activities.

Great salesmen often mirror altogether naturally, without ever a thought. If their prospect speaks with an accent, they take on a hint of a similar accent of their own. If the prospect speaks softly, they do, too. If he sprawls in his chair, they take on a like posture. Connection is enhanced.

Mirroring can feel unnatural at first, but if you practice it, with your focus on the other person instead of yourself, you'll find that it quickly becomes easy. It helps not only how you're received, but also how effectively you listen. Make it a part of your interpersonal skill base and natural style. It will pay off in multiple ways, for everything from discussing house rules with your teenager to winning the last million dollars in a multimillion-dollar deal.

Years ago, in my Big 8 CPA firm days, I attended a new seminar every year for some sort of management or leadership style analysis and coaching. I learned what "type" of style I had under at least a half-dozen different nomenclatures. Whether it was a "Q-1" or "A B" or "11:00," or whatever that particular system "named" each style, the meaning of the labels typically focused upon people vs. task orientation, introversion vs. extroversion, and other various behavioral spectra.

In the end, almost every one of these analysis systems sought to tell us how to better deal with others who operated under different styles—emphasizing those with different focuses or priorities from our own. We learned that the aggressive speaker with enthusiastic gestures and direct style might have difficulty communicating with the quiet, reserved person. I, being the friendly, direct, and inordinately enthusiastic type, learned that for some people I needed to pipe down in order to be best appreciated. No gestures. Quiet voice. No intrusion into the other person's space. Fact-oriented discussions, with references to instinctive or emotional factors left out.

In one particularly difficult relationship of those days, with one superior, my relationship improved literally overnight when I began to communicate in his style. He was the quiet, reserved, and all-quantitative-fact type, so I adapted to his style. I was quiet, purely factual, and tidy and contained in my every communication with him. He commented about eight months after I started focusing attention to style that I had improved in technical performance amazingly in a very short time. He said I had grown more technically in the last eight months than I had in the preceding eight years.

In reality I'm sure I was no better technically. I simply had finally learned how to talk with him in a way that was comfortable enough for him to hear. That was the year I made partner with my Big 8 CPA firm, and his support may well have put me over the top.

129

STRATEGIC ANGER

In the course of negotiations it almost never pays to openly demonstrate anger. *I actually have become so accustomed to controlling and monitoring anger that I found myself automatically turning on the calm recently when I was abruptly cut off in traffic by an overly anxious driver slipping through a red light. The anger automatically caused me to mask my reaction, and to think quickly. I smiled and waved. His grouchy face turned immediately to a confused smile as he waved back. I'm sure he wondered who that friend or neighbor was that he had cut off in traffic. It completely changed a most irritating moment to absolute fun.*

Generally the objective is to remain calm and cool, even in the face of enormous adversity. However, sometimes when those on the other side of the table cross over certain types of lines, a brief but intense show of hostility is warranted—and, yes, even required.

The moment to show the flair of anger may be:

1. When needed as a protective device, to shield others, or

2. When the opponent has wantonly failed to show a sense of quid pro quo for a qualified concession you have granted.

Anger can be appropriate as the last-ditch protective or defensive device. If one party to the transaction has been unduly attacked or criticized by the opponent, and the person attacked is essential to happy settlement of the deal, it may be time to set down a foot, loudly. The victim of the attack can't be the one to draw the line in the sand. Anything he says or does in response to the attack will look weak.

At the same time, the attacker must be made to understand clearly that he has stepped into dangerous territory. Sometimes intensely angry reactions, by anyone **except** the subject of the attack, can do a far better job of putting the attacker in his place.

At the tail end of an important negotiation several years ago, our client and I had chosen what we felt was a "best" offer among many. We had agreed to a sit-down-and-work-through-the-issues meeting, to try to come to resolution on the remaining points. During the course of the discussion the buyer made a highly insulting remark, impugning the character of my client. I "felt" my client's face darken in rage. I saved him from having an outburst by having it myself, in full and flaming glory. I said, in effect, "How dare you!", with rage and passion. I tiraded on for several moments in magnificent fury. The buyers blanched, and became tight-lipped and sullen at my accusations. At the end was an awkward silence.

My client finally broke the silence with, "I'm hungry. How about a lunch break?" Everyone in the room (except me— remaining dutifully angry) laughed with relief. At lunch my client told me that he was just about to tell the buyer to jump in a lake. (His words were more colorful—I'm being civilized for polite publication). He said that he appreciated my defense and that he probably couldn't have gotten past this without those things having been said. Now he felt better able to listen calmly and to evaluate their actions in the next phase of discussions far more rationally and comfortably.

The buyer opened the meeting after lunch with an immediate and frank apology. He said he understood that all of our actions to date had been entirely in good faith and that the tensions of the day had simply overcome his rational perception for a moment. My client accepted his apology with calm goodwill and grace, and the discussions proceeded. The remainder of the negotiations came off without a hitch—with impressive even-temperedness and reasonableness on both sides of the table.

The second circumstance in which anger may be appropriate involves unexpected reneging by the opposing negotiators on an issue where a clearly implied quid pro quo was in order. Successful negotiations require some sense of give and take for both sides. If a stated concession, or even a strongly implied concession, is withdrawn after your acquiescence has been confirmed, the balance becomes off-center. The disingenuous party must be challenged. Resistance is in order. Bully tactics cannot be permitted. They will inevitably multiply. Undeserved acquiescence screams weakness. The buyer will know that there are more weak retreats where that one came from.

Cashing In!

Instead of mildly accepting, the seller must step forward bluntly and, with a measured bit of anger, say, "I'm sorry, but that really doesn't work for me."

All of this said, be forewarned that as negotiations for sale of a business continue for a prolonged time period, tension will increase, and it will become inevitably more tempting to react with anger. My mother told me, *"Everyone is entitled to stupid remarks sometimes. The problem is that some people abuse the privilege."* I find myself thinking of that bit of wisdom often in the final, tense stages of any negotiation. Nevertheless, I squelch my anger, unless it's genuinely needed to make a point.

Think before you speak. *The trouble with talking too fast is that you may say something you haven't thought of yet.*

LISTENING

Sages through the ages have known the power of great listening. *It has often been said that the best way to win an argument is with your ears—not with your mouth.*

With any negotiation, it is critical to get a thorough understanding of what the other side wants and values most in the deal. Obviously the buyer wants to pay less and the seller wants him to pay more. However, there's so much more to the tapestry of a deal. Why does the buyer want the deal? What are the real triggers to his desire? Does he need additional sales volume? Does the geography have appeal? Is there a fervent desire to take this opportunity away from some competitor? Is the chief buyer's job at risk if he doesn't complete this acquisition? Understanding the core elements of the buyer's desire will allow the negotiator to know what pieces of the deal are likely to be non-negotiable, and what pieces may be flexible. These elements also give the negotiator tips on how to heighten the buyer's desire throughout the process.

Great listeners hear the subtleties. One must have a firm grasp of subtleties to practice great dealsmanship.

When I was a youngster in the negotiating world, I heard the comment on more than one occasion that I had great peripheral vision. This compliment meant that I had a good eye for the small things. I had a tendency to notice the acute interest (or fear) in the eyes of the opposition on some little issue, which we may have assumed to be unimportant. I could also feel the forward momentum in the midst of the negotiation when we reached that magical point where we were close enough to satisfy the opposition. I had good instincts about how much was enough, which allowed me to make good judgments about when to stand firm and wait for the other side to acquiesce.

Most people can focus only on one thing at a time. *Have you ever noticed that when you're driving and looking carefully for an address, you turn down the volume on the radio?* You are adjusting to allow yourself full intensity of attention on what you're doing. When you're speaking during a negotiation, you're concentrating intensely upon what you have to say. However, to be a great negotiator you must simultaneously pay tremendous attention to how the listener is receiving your message. Also, when the other side speaks, shut up and listen with great intensity and with all antennae up.

Listening well offers additional advantages, even beyond what you hear. *A closed mouth gathers no foot.* When we're tense, and there's an overly long pause, it can be tempting to fill it. Rarely do pertinent or appropriate comments come from "filler." *Abraham Lincoln said, "Better to remain silent and thought a fool, than to speak out, and remove all doubt."* I like that.

Strong listening skills and acute peripheral vision can be a tremendous advantage in the negotiating arena, and are well worth careful cultivation for the aspiring negotiator. Listen and benefit.

PLAYBACK

We have all heard of empathetic listening techniques wherein you "playback," in your own words, what a speaker has just said to you. The object of this exercise is to confirm that you have heard and understood correctly. In a negotiating scenario, this can be a highly effective communication style.

First, it does the clear job of confirmation. If you play it back, but miss, your listener can hear what he has conveyed, and can correct any misconceptions.

In an intense negotiation, however, this technique actually does a great deal more psychologically.

My first meaningful exposure to the effective use of this technique was in negotiating for the purchase of a division company for one of my clients. Our objective was to make the buy aggressively and directly, without allowing the seller to actively pit us against a range of competitive buyers.

As I spoke with the lead negotiator for the seller, I found him frequently using a playback technique to verify his understanding of the positions I had taken. This had a couple of interesting and somewhat difficult-to-handle impacts.

First of all, my emotional response to his generally accurate recaps of our position was to feel that he was very fair-minded. He clearly was listening, and he seemed to be giving some level of fair recognition to my points, just by voicing them back. Accordingly, he seemed to be trying to understand my point of view. This made it hard to play rough with him. Somehow it felt inequitable or unfair not to reciprocate with honest appreciation of his position as well.

Secondly, the same style of fair-minded recap was selectively used to point out the magnitude of the things I was asking for. He said, "You think the company is worth X. We think it's worth Y. You would like for us to commit to sale at X now, without further testing our position in the marketplace, by courting competitive bids. Is that right?"

Me, awkwardly: "Ah...yes."

Seller: "We would love to finish this transaction quickly and easily without a full-blown shopping of the company to other buyers, but we really don't want to do that at X dollars. We need to either climb to a price where we feel confident that we're close to market, or postpone further discussions with your client until we've had time to at least probe the marketplace."

Drat. Nice save.

We raised our bid, and quickly closed the deal at a handsome price to the seller. My buyer client made great use of the new business, and did well with the acquisition in spite of the high price, but I was frustrated by my inability to attain the company for him at a bargain purchase price.

In spite of the increase in pricing which the seller achieved, we did get the deal closed, which, in this case, was critical—almost regardless of price. Without the seller's calm, cool playback technique, I'm not sure we would ever have gotten to closure. For others in the transaction, like me, the disarming directness and sense of goodwill from that repeatedly fair playback of our position made a huge difference. It helped tremendously to make my client and me feel that we were being treated reasonably, in spite of tough pricing.

AVOIDING THE TELLS

In poker playing there is a phenomenon known by the pros as "watching for the tells." Tells are subtle indicators of thought which typically include eye movements, facial expressions, or body posture, consistently shown by a given player in a given situation. The player with the especially powerful hand may always lean back a bit and guard visibility of his hand more carefully than normal. The player who draws a losing two or three cards may hold unusually still and concentrate on his cards very intently, as if by studying his hand more carefully, he will prevent himself from displaying his disappointment.

In negotiating a deal, there are likewise subtle signs of acceptance or disappointment with proposed terms. Unlike the poker player, the deal negotiator may not have the opportunity to see the other side in action repeatedly. Accordingly, the reaction to the tell must be much quicker, and based on an almost intuitive read of much subtler signs.

Several years ago I was working with a client on a buy-side project. My client wanted to make an offer on a manufacturing company that was being marketed by that company's attorney. The attorney was conducting a limited-auction type sale and would not tip us about his client's pricing expectations. I knew *that offers had already been submitted, and that we were late in the process. My client felt that the business was probably worth about $40 million for net stock. I was concerned that we might be able to get by with a lower purchase price than the $40 million contemplated offer. My suggestion would have been to start at $30-35 million. However, the client was worried about missing the deal, and asked me to move forward with an offer at the $40 million mark.*

To make the offer, I set a face-to-face appointment with the attorney, with the explanation that I would be in his city anyway and I simply preferred to discuss the matter in person. In reality, my visit was not so casual. I felt that I needed to have the advantage of seeing his reaction to my proposal. The moment I mentioned $40 million, I saw him glance down and quickly mask all expression. I knew instinctively from his reaction that we were high. I immediately moved to correct my overzealous bid. I went on to explain that this price would be for gross assets only, and that the seller would, of course, have to pay back his approximately $15 million in liabilities from the $40 million proceeds. This took our $40 million bid down to $25 million in one sentence.

I saw a quick mental calculation flash across his face, as he said "Okay...I see." I could tell that we were still in the running. He then began to ask for clarification on other points of the deal, like employment contracts, noncompete agreements, etc. Quick change of topic in this manner is often a way to try to distance oneself from the point last mentioned (price, in this case). People tend to do this when they are worried about their reaction being too visible to the opposition. His desire to move quickly to the other details of our proposal reinforced my certainty about the adequacy of our price. Accordingly, I responded as hard line as possible on all of the remaining points.

The deal which I took back to my buyer client was $15 million less than he had originally been willing to pay, and with far superior terms in a number of ways. The deal closed a fast thirty days later, and our client was delighted.

As a seller, remember: if at all possible, it is always prudent to avoid receiving a verbal presentation of the buyer's proposal. The written proposal gives you time to consider before responding, and avoids the risk of the opposition's analysis of your reaction. If a written presentation is impossible to arrange and you're forced into a face-to-face meeting, be careful.

Try to be a little unpredictable in response in order to muddy the other side's ability to read your reaction. Vary the pace. React slowly on one point. Move in a quick, no–thought manner on the next. Pause—maybe even a little too long sometimes. Erratic timing makes it difficult to read the emotional content of your response. Choose your words carefully. Guard your posture and expressions, but don't freeze or be unnatural, and thus obvious in your control.

Generally, the more you can convey uncertainty, reluctance, or "close call, but probably not" in your response, the more the buyer is likely to solidify details in your favor. Be mysterious. *Put on your Mona Lisa face. (Yes—guys can have that, too!)*

The less the opposition can read into reactions about any element of the proposed terms, the better your negotiating position will be.

MEETING IN THE MIDDLE

There's a natural inclination, when trying to reach a compromise solution, to "split it down the middle." Such a split has an automatic appearance or feeling of fairness.

If I, as a seller, want the noncompete agreement to run for one year, but you, as the buyer, have a five-year agreement in mind, it may well be fairly easy to get both of us to a three-year mid-point. If I ask for $12 million for my company and you offer $10 million, $11 million would "feel" like the fair compromise solution.

Accordingly, in the case where the mid-point value might be acceptable, or even desirable, this natural mid-point compromise mentality can be a very good thing. All too often, however, negotiators will find themselves in a situation where meeting at the halfway point is simply not an acceptable solution.

In those instances, I would suggest several things. First of all, this is probably not an advantageous moment to continue the discussion on the numerical issue at odds. Change the subject. Although some "you were there and I was here" mentality may naturally be played back to you by the opposition later, you will have a far better chance of veering away from the split-in-the-middle solution if you sidestep and steer away from the issue.

Consider the possibility of reshuffling the deck altogether, and changing the elements of bidding. If it's possible to take an extremely different tack, and actually change other key elements to the deal (such as what will be included in the sale), that may jolt things enough to make prior discussions about the numbers irrelevant. With luck, it may force you to start anew.

Alternatively, you might consider focusing upon other issues as if they were as important or even more important than the numeric starting point under discussion. That may give you the opportunity to re-approach the troublesome number later from a different tack. After you're well into the discussion of the diversionary point, it will be far easier to revisit your rationale for a completely different pricing mechanism.

For example, in the midst of a tense discussion about pricing of an offer, the seller might shift gears with an entirely new issue. "This employment contract is really a big issue for me. I've been told that I would probably have to commit to six months or a year transition. Your proposal, with a three-year employment requirement, simply puts us in another environment altogether."

As you chip away at other issues and become more distant from the numeric point of contention, a clean re-approach becomes simpler and more likely to be feasible.

Sometimes however, it's impossible to avoid having the other side come back to you with a protest that you aren't being fair because you're not considering his even-handed "split" solution. As a last resort, there may be no way to avoid drawing a clear line in the sand. "I'm sorry, but this is one of those situations where a split down the middle just won't work. The bottom line is that your offer simply isn't competitive at those numbers."

(Smack! Ouch!)

Of course, be as gentle, as sincere, and as straightforward as possible in delivering such news.

When meeting in the middle simply can't work, you must either: (a) find the creative solution, (b) force the other side to rise to the occasion, or (c) back away. It's one of the toughest tests of high-end negotiating skills. *As Benjamin Franklin observed more than two hundred years ago, "One of the great secrets of life is in learning to make stepping stones out of stumbling blocks."*

GOOD COP/BAD COP

There is a technique known the world over, which is a classic in the negotiating arena. It's most often called something like "Good Cop/Bad Cop," in acknowledgment of the age-old police method of getting information. One negotiator is kind, reasonable and warm. His partner is mean-spirited and harsh in every way. The prisoner is nurtured toward a trusting relationship with the Good Cop. The trust is enhanced and built far more rapidly, by injection of the counterforce in the form of the notorious Bad Cop. Bad Cop attacks and belittles. Good Cop protects and sees reason. Prisoner becomes at ease with Good Cop, begins to feel indebted to Good Cop. He soon begins to confide and trust in Good Cop.

Teamwork is essential. It gives them someone else to shoot at.
One of the fascinating things about Good Cop/Bad Cop in a negotiating scenario is that it often can work quite effectively, even when all parties to the discussion know exactly what game is being played. The negotiator in the "prisoner" role has the opportunity to use the Good Cop sessions as a forum to vent. He can offer possible compromise solutions without losing face. He can threaten to cut off discussions without needing to go so far as to walk away. He can generally convey things more openly to the Good Cop, without overtly committing to a fixed

position. Prisoner: "I'm afraid if Bad Cop goes one step further on that issue, it will leave me with no choice but complete withdrawal."

The Good Cop simultaneously has the opportunity to put forth predictions of the likely results of the proposed actions. Good Cop: "I'll bet if you offered to personally guarantee the debt, Bad Cop would have to soften on his hard stance about insisting on all cash for this deal."

The entire interplay in the Good Cop—Bad Cop game is a mechanism for setting up fronts, communicating positions, and exploring alternatives. Bad Cop defines the hard-line stance, while Good Cop is the sympathetic problem solver.

It's a wonderful game!

THE BLUFF

There are times in the life of the negotiator when you will find
yourself playing poker for big stakes with only a pair of deuces
in hand. You may have no choice but to mask your fear, hold
your chin high, and forge ahead.

*Our firm was representing a national trade magazine in possi-
ble sale. The magazine was owned and published by a not-for-
profit trade association that was in dire straits. The association was out of money, six months overdue on its rents for a
substantial space, and besieged with criticism by its con-
stituent members.*

*In surveying the trade association's holdings, we quickly deter-
mined that one of their assets of potential value was the national magazine publication. Although the magazine had consistently lost money for the association for ten-plus years, the revenue base was good, with premium advertisers at good margins. The verified subscriber count was focused and excellent,
and it clearly looked like a venture which, within an independent for-profit environment, could be strongly profitable.*

*As we explored possible suitors for the business, we quickly
came to realize that there were only two "natural" suitors with*

likelihood of strong interest. This publication catered to a niche market where there were clearly two dominant players competing for access to readers.

Very early in the process one of the two best suitors dropped out due to internal problems. We kept several other possible second-tier contenders alive in the deal, to try to hold the feeling of competition. However, in reality, we knew that we were down to one real contender.

When the bids came in, less than two months after we were originally hired, the one "best" buyer was more than five times higher than the next runner-up.

We knew that this buyer would never have bid so heartily had they not feared the competition of the other big player in their niche. We did not tell them who the bidders were, or where they stood relatively. In order to solidify the feeling of competitive pressure, we insisted on maintaining our right to continue to discuss the sale with multiple suitors. In spite of the protests of our "best" buyer, we refused to enter into any form of "stop-shop" (commitment to exclusivity) until agreement on the final definitive purchase document and completion of their due diligence.

Things proceeded rapidly, until about one week before we were scheduled to wrap up the transaction. At this last moment a problem was found regarding the association's title to a portion of its subscriber list.

The buyer said that this issue created a major problem for them, and changed their mind about their original pricing. Given this issue, they felt that they needed to lower their price by 20%.

Our instincts screamed that any concession in pricing at this late stage in the discussions would be a blatant acknowledgment of weakness. We feared that if we allowed such a precipitous drop in pricing, further drops would almost certainly follow.

We told the buyer that the deal was off. We said we would go back to the other bidders rather than accept such a change. We said that we were sorry, but that we did not believe other buyers would expect this issue to lower price to any significant extent. Accordingly, if they insisted on pressing this issue, we would simply have to abandon their proposal and return to the other buyers.

Our client was shocked and dismayed, and panicked at our response. This offer was more than five times greater than the next runner-up, and they did not want to lose it. We explained that we believed that the buyer would lose faith in the overall deal immediately if they realized that their competition was not in the hunt. Furthermore, we believed that acceptance of such changes to the deal could well tip them off about the weakness of the competition, and thus foil their appetite entirely. We finally convinced our client to remain silent, calm, and firm for at least three days, while the buyer contemplated alternatives.

Thankfully, we didn't need three days, as it turned out. Six hours after our original "No" response, the buyer called us and said, "Never mind. We're back on at the original price." We closed the deal one week later, as originally scheduled for an all-cash price that was magnificent.

CONCLUSION

In representing business owners in sale, we often find ourselves wishing that we could meet every client several years in advance of sale, to preview their business's value, and coach them about posturing for sale. Readers of this book obviously are thinking ahead about sale, and have a chance to prepare in advance. Analyze value. Think about strengths and how to capitalize on them, and take strategic action to shore up weaknesses. The right strategic moves, several years in advance of sale, can add substantially to value. Plan and posture ahead of time, to optimize the fruits of your labor.

When you begin to suspect that the time for sale is right, keep your eyes open for the opportune moment. If a downturn is in sight, jump ahead of it to make your move. When great things are popping in every direction, sell the picture of superstar performance to come. To achieve optimum results, you can't be hesitant to jump in quickly, when you sense that the timing is right in making the move to sell.

Remember that it's far too important for the handyman, do-it-yourself approach. Hire a highly skilled, quality, professional firm to assist you. The cost is not negligible, but invariably the return on that cost in terms of incremental price attained will be many times the fee.

You've taken a powerful first step. You're preparing! *The first step to doing anything successfully is to become interested in it.* You're on the way to a fat and lucrative sale!

As the owner, builder, and investor in your business endeavor, you have earned the right to cash in well. You will sell your business only one time, and the reward for that one closing could and should be the grand slam of your business career. Sell well, live long, and prosper!

Appendices

Appendix A

GLOSSARY OF MIDDLE MARKET MERGER AND ACQUISITION TERMS

AAA. American Arbitration Association

Acquisition corporation. A separate corporate entity established for the purpose of being the holding company for a given acquisition or acquisitions (typically utilized to protect assets of the buying owners from legal action in the event of problems, and/or to accomplish certain tax objectives)

Affiliate. A secondary party related by virtue of commonality of ownership, family relationship, or other connections which create common interests

Arbitration. An agreed-upon procedure for resolving disputes outside of formal legal proceedings (the resulting arbitrator's decisions may be binding or nonbinding, depending upon agreement of parties in advance)

Asset purchase. The purchase of named assets (and potentially the assumption of named liabilities) of a company (as opposed to a stock purchase, where only outstanding stock ownership is transferred)

Bad faith. Any action done with the intent to deceive or mislead

Basket. A commonly used "reserve" device to accumulate claims in an ongoing tally, for eventual payment or reimbursement if certain aggregate thresholds or criteria are met (may be either reimbursement of amounts beyond the threshold, or a trigger of first-dollar reimbursement if the thresholds are met)

Business broker. An agent who facilitates purchase or sale, usually for a percentage of price to be paid upon successful closure

Call option. An option contract that gives the holder the right, but not the obligation, to buy a certain quantity of an underlying security from the writer of the option, at a specified price, up to a specified date

Closing. The finalizing of the sale of a company in which the ownership is transferred from the seller to the buyer

Collar. Combinations of put options and call options that can limit, within a specific range, the risk that investment shares will drop in value (also generally limits potential for increased value)

Collateral position. A security interest in specific named assets

Confidentiality agreement. A written agreement providing for secrecy between parties, and prohibiting use of confidential information by third parties; often provides for restriction of use beyond a specific named purpose (such as evaluation of potential purchase)

Contingent liabilities. Possible future liabilities which may result in costs or damages if certain events occur

Contingent payment. A future payment which will only be required if certain conditions are satisfied

Conversion privilege. The right to convert one contractual right or privilege to another (for example, preferred stock which may be convertible to notes payable, or to common stock)

Cross guarantee. Guarantees by multiple parties to secure the same indebtedness

Deed of trust. A document used in some states instead of a mortgage; title is held by a trustee until the debt is satisfied and the deed of trust is released

Definitive Agreement. The final governing agreement stipulating all detailed terms of an acquisition (also called the Definitive Purchase Agreement)

Diminimus rule. A provision for ignoring a certain contract provision if the financial impact is less than some stated threshold level

Due diligence. The process of investigation, performed by the prospective buyers, into the details of a potential investment, such as the examination of financial data, operations and management, and the verification of material facts

Earnings, multiple of. A mechanism for business valuation which takes some measure of earnings (commonly either net earnings, earnings before interest and taxes, or earnings before interest, taxes, depreciation and amortization) and applies a "multiplier" to those earnings to arrive at enterprise value

Earnout. A special additional benefit provision for supplemental payments to seller post-closing, to be paid only if certain specific financial or operating targets are met

EBIT. Earnings before interest and taxes

EBITDA. Earnings before interest, taxes, depreciation, and amortization

EBT. Earnings before taxes

Enterprise value. A measure of the market value of a company's ongoing operations

Equity fund. An investment fund established for the purpose of buying equity interests in companies

Escrow agreement. An agreement which governs the use and distribution of funds or securities held or set aside pending resolution of certain specified matters

Escrow fund. Money or securities deposited with a neutral third party, to be delivered upon fulfillment of certain conditions established by an escrow agreement

ESOP. Employee stock ownership plan; a tax-deferred retirement-benefit plan for employee ownership of a company, subject to ERISA regulations

Exclusivity agreement. An agreement whereby a seller promises to limit discussions or negotiations with only a single buyer

Extraordinary item. An unusual and non-recurring event which materially affected a company's finances in a reporting period

Financial buyer. An equity-fund buyer which purchases companies, usually for stand-alone operation, to produce return on investment for its shareholders at above-average return rates, in exchange for the above-average risk of business ownership (generally not a "strategic buyer")

Financing. The borrowing of funds

Finder. An intermediary who generally provides limited services of finding a buyer or seller in an acquisition transaction

First collateral. The dominant security interest when multiple financing parties are providing funding for the same transaction, or for purchase of similar or related assets

For cause. Done in response to a specific incident or incidents (for example, termination was "for cause" because the terminated employee committed theft or fraud)

Grandfather provision. Allowable continuance of a practice that is now forbidden

Gross price. The total price a buyer pays before expenses, commission, or other costs

Hedge. To take an action in order to reduce the risk of adverse price movements in an asset (a hedge on public stock received in sale might limit the seller's risk in accepting stock versus cash)

Holdback. A contractual condition in which payment is withheld until a specific event occurs

Horizontal acquisition. Purchase of a company which is either a direct competitor, or which, by its nature, could supply similar goods or services to some segment of the marketplace

Indemnification. A promise to protect a counterparty from damages resulting from misrepresentations or certain named actions or conditions

Intermediary. A third party who facilitates a deal between two parties

Investment banker. An individual or institution which acts as an underwriter, advisor or agent for corporations or individuals in investment-related transactions

IPO. Initial public offering; the first sale of stock by a company to the general public or to investors

Knowledge qualifier. A provision which restricts a specific representation or warranty to be effective only if the representing party actually had knowledge of the matter at hand

Letter of Intent. A preliminary agreement of good faith intent to move toward consummation of a buy/sell transaction

Letter of Interest. A preliminary expression of expected value and possible purchase terms for a potential acquisition; also referred to occasionally as "expression of interest"

Lien. A legal claim against an asset which is used to secure a loan or a lease

Market value adjustment. An adjustment to current estimated market values, encompassing changes in the market climate or business fluctuations

Material information. Information which is highly significant to value or to some other business judgment

Mezzanine financing. Late-stage financing (such as bids, warrants, preferred stock, or other) with both debt-like and equity-like characteristics; generally more expensive and more risky than senior debt, but less costly and less risky than equity capital

Mirroring. Mimicking the communication style of another person in order to establish greater rapport

Misrepresentation. Intentional concealment or distortion of information in order to deceive or mislead

Nondisclosure agreement. A written agreement providing for secrecy between parties, and prohibiting use of confidential information by third parties; often provides for restriction of use beyond a specific named purpose (such as evaluation of potential purchase)

No-shop. An agreement whereby a seller promises to continue discussions or negotiations exclusively with one buyer

Note. A written agreement to repay debt

Option. The right, but not the obligation, to buy (call option) or sell (put option)

Personal guarantee. A promise made by a guarantor which obligates him/her to personally repay specifically guaranteed debts in the event of default

Phase I (environmental review). The first-level environmental review, typically involving site inspection, inquiries about practices and procedures, and review of governmental (EPA, sewer authority, etc.) and other records of historic environmental issues

Phase II (environmental review). The second-level environmental review, usually initiated when there is a concern about a particular possible problem, and usually involving some specific site testing (soil samples, water testing, etc.)

Post-closing adjustment. A price adjustment made after closing, usually pursuant to specific terms set forth in the Definitive Purchase Agreement

Post-closing audit. An audit performed after the closing, usually a financial audit done as of the closing date

Pre-closing. Events prior to the final closing date; may refer to a meeting shortly before a scheduled closing, the purpose of which is to walk through all documentation and make sure all is in order for a scheduled closing (i.e., a pre-closing may be scheduled one day ahead of the closing date)

Present value. The current value of future cash payments, discounted at an appropriate interest or "discount" rate

Proceeds. Money received through a specific financial event, such as a sale or loan

Put option. An option contract that gives the holder the right, but not the obligation, to sell a certain quantity of an underlying security at a specified price up to a specified date

Representation. A statement promising truth or fullness of disclosure with respect to a named matter

Second deed of trust. A specified collateral interest, secondary to a primary secured party's first claim

Secrecy agreement. A written agreement providing for secrecy between parties

Security interest. The legal interest of a creditor in assets or real property perfected through the filings under the uniform commercial code and/or through the filing of a mortgage which establishes the creditor's right to the assets or property in the event of default on behalf of the debtor

Senior lender. Lender with the first collateral position on assets, usually a traditional bank, and usually the largest secured lender

Shell corporation. A corporate entity established solely for a given purpose, usually with little or no net worth except as may be input for an express purpose

Stand still agreement. An agreement sometimes required by a lender, which limits the rights of others to foreclose on any security interests they may have in the same assets; also, a term used loosely to refer to an exclusivity agreement (the seller will "stand still," and cease talks with alternative buyers)

Stop-shop. An agreement whereby a seller promises to continue discussions or negotiations exclusively with one buyer

Strategic buyer. A buyer which is an operating company in a related area of business, usually with interest in a given acquisition due to some type of likely synergy from the business combination

Surviving contract provision. A contract provision which will continue to remain effective after the rest of the contract has expired

Time value of money. The idea that a dollar now is worth more than a dollar in the future

Triple net lease. A lease wherein the lessee is solely responsible for all of the costs relating to the asset being leased (taxes, insurance, maintenance, etc.)

Valuation reserve. An allowance or contra-asset established to provide for an anticipated diminishment in value of an asset (such as a reserve on inventories, to provide an allowance for unsaleable or obsolete items)

Vertical acquisition. Purchase of a company which is or which, by its nature, could be a supplier to or customer of the buyer (said to be an "upstream" or a "downstream" acquisition, respectively)

Warranty. A statement guaranteeing the validity of a certain assertion or representation

Note: The above definitions are intended to provide a general business understanding of the terms as most commonly used in middle market merger and acquisition discussions. Specific legal implications may differ depending on context, so always consult with legal advisors, and be attentive to contract-specific definitions within any agreement.

Appendix B

SAMPLE NONDISCLOSURE AGREEMENT

The undersigned hereby agrees:

That all information, data and materials disclosed or furnished (herein called the Information) relating to Douglas Group (hereinafter Douglas) client AB123 (herein called the Company) will be maintained strictly confidential and that, in consideration for such disclosure, no use of the Information will be made by any signing party, or employees of such party, other than for internal evaluation purposes, on a strictly confidential basis.

It is understood that disclosure of any of the Information, including the possibility that the Shareholders may consider sale, disclosure of the current status of the Company, or disclosure of any information to customers, vendors, competitors, or employees of the Company would cause serious financial damage to the Company and/or its affiliates.

Further, the undersigned agrees not to copy, duplicate, disclose or deliver all or any portion of the Information to a third party or permit any third party to inspect, copy or duplicate the same. Additionally, the undersigned understands and agrees that all inquiries regarding the Company shall be made through Douglas, and no contact shall be made directly to the Company offices.

This shall not, however, prevent the undersigned from disclosing to others or using in any manner:

1. Information which has been published and has become part of the public domain other than by acts or omissions by the receiving party.

2. Information which has been furnished or made known to the undersigned by third parties as a matter of right without restriction of disclosure, or

3. Information which the undersigned can show was already in its possession at the time it entered into this Agreement and which was not acquired directly or indirectly from the Company, their employees or their representatives

This agreement shall remain in effect for a term of two years from the execution date hereof and upon request, the receiving party will promptly return all data and materials furnished by Douglas and destroy any internal analyses and/or workpapers related to the evaluation of the Company.

Signature _____ Date _____

Name (please print)_____ Title _____

Company _____ Phone_____

Address _____ Fax _____

City, State, Zip _____ E-mail _____

Appendix C

SELLER INFORMATION CHECKLIST

General Information

- Narrative overview - Description of key aspects of business; Executive summary

- Financial overview -
    Recap of key financial indicators
    Most recent three-five years, and sometimes forward projections

Financial Data

- Pertinent recast financial information
    Owners' compensation
    Unusual or nonrecurring costs
    Family or personal discretionary expenses

- Audited financial statements - usually past three-five years

- Internal financial statements - usually most recent year-to-date

- Gross margin analysis - history of margins by major product or service segment

Markets

- Brochures

- Market potential overview - discussion of major areas of potential growth

- Sales by market - history and trends by business market segment

- Major competitors

- Sales by territory - history and trends by geographic or territorial segment

- Analysis of sales channels - sytems utilized, use of inside staff, reps, etc.

- Customer dependency analysis - often top ten customer volumes without specific identification (to permit buyer analysis of percentage dependency on largest few)

- Backlog reports - preferably comparable with past periods

- Pending new opportunities - description of significant add-on possibilities pending

Facilities and Equipment

- Facilities overview

- Real estate appraisals

- Equipment listings

- Equipment appraisals

- Technology / systems / computer overview

- Capital expenditure needs analysis

People

- Organizational chart

- Management-level staffing - descriptions of backgrounds for top-level managers

- Staff summary - description of employee titles, counts, and pay scales

- Recap of employee benefit plans

Appendix D

BUYER SOURCING
CHECKLIST

General

- General search for companies in right industry / right size (multiple accessible sources by SIC code)

- Research of Merger and Acquisition paid databases

- Equity fund buyers

- General acquisition research of periodicals and newspapers (recent histories of major transactions)

- Buyer intermediaries (valid source, but exercise caution: many send out mass mailings with thinly veiled description)

Industry specific

- Officers and executives of trade associations

- Editors and reporters of trade magazines

- Industry expert professionals: CPAs, attorneys, and consultants who specialize in the industry *

---

* Excellent sources of information but require hands-on individual contact and conversation in order to gain meaningful data

- Top company lists provided by business journals and trade periodicals

Company specific

- Competitors

- Major equipment suppliers*

- Raw material suppliers*

- Suppliers of adjacent goods or services to same customer base

---

* Excellent sources of information but require hands-on individual contact and conversation in order to gain meaningful data

Appendix E

DEFINITIVE AGREEMENT
SHORT FORM
CHECKLIST

Purchase Price

Cash
Form of other consideration
Definition of what is being purchased
Releases from seller personal guarantees
Other agreements required for transaction
> (i.e., consulting, employment, noncompetes,
> collateral)

Deferred Purchase Payments

Amounts
Collateral
Guarantees
Definition of contingencies
Timing of payments

Deposit

Amount required
Forfeiture privileges
Escrow requirements
Stop-shop

Timing

Closing date
Access to information during interim
Backout privileges

Representations and Warranties

Seller:
Clear title
Honesty and material accuracy (include critical
information as exhibits: financial statements,
key contracts, etc.)
Normal conduct of business
Has informed buyer of important matters or
contingencies (enumerate)

Buyer:
Financial statements presented to seller
are accurate (important if seller used such
statements to assess financial viability of buyer)

Material adverse events - definition and consequences
Intermediary fees
Cooperative transfer of contracts
Indemnifications
Other transaction-specific matters
Arbitration or dispute-resolution process

Employment / Consulting

Time required
Nature of work
Payment timing
Benefits (vacation, health care)

Appendix F

EMPLOYMENT AGREEMENT
CHECKLIST

Fundamental Terms

> Duration of commitment / renewal defined
> Salary or base and mechanisms or formula for
>   periodic change, if applicable
> Bonus arrangements clearly defined, and mechanisms
>   or formula for periodic change, if applicable
> Benefits, vacation, retirement, car, and any other fringes

Duties

> Authority / title / responsibilities
> Ability to transfer (geographically) or not
> Board position, if applicable

Termination

> For cause, clearly defined
> Employer discretionary "performance" termination
>   rights
> Employee discretionary rights to terminate
> Notice requirements
> Impact of partial year on bonus/benefits
> Change of control rights (in event of company sale)

Confidentiality / Noncompetes

Confidentiality situations
Noncompete time period, if applicable
Definition of noncompetes (restricted to customers?
　　restricted to principal area of business worked in?)
Restrictions on taking/hiring employees

Special Incentives

Bonus on sale, if applicable
Salary continuation, or other golden parachute provisions
Moving expenses, if applicable

Stock Rights

Stock buy-back provisions in the event of termination
Impact on pending stock rights (options, warranties,
　　etc.) if employment terminates, or if company is sold

About the Author

Deborah L. Douglas is President and CEO of the Douglas Group, one of the leaders today in middle market mergers and acquisitions. The firm has been extremely successful, creating great wealth for business owners, and powerful business combinations in a wide range of industries.

Ms. Douglas is a former audit partner and Director of Merger and Acquisition Activities for one of the then "Big Eight" CPA firms, before forming Douglas Group in 1989. She has been a dedicated and energetic contributor in civic and community affairs, and is a popular and frequent speaker at a wide range of industry, trade, and general business events.

For additional information about Ms. Douglas or about the firm, visit their Web site at DouglasGroup.net, or e-mail DDouglas@DouglasGroup.net.